THE WEARSID[illegible]MPIONS

THE WEARSIDE CHAMPIONS

Archie Potts

1993
BEWICK PRESS
TYNE AND WEAR

To Margaret

First published in Great Britain by
Bewick Press
132 Claremont Road
Whitley Bay
Tyne and Wear
NE26 3TX

ISBN 0-9516056-8-2

Printed and bound in Great Britain by Mayfair Print Group, William Street, Sunderland SR1 1UL.

CONTENTS

INTRODUCTION

I was seven years old when I saw my first boxing match. This was in 1939. My Uncle Stan was a boyhood friend of the Sunderland flyweight boxer, Mickey O'Neill, and my uncle took me along with him to see O'Neill box. Mickey was one of the Gill brothers, a family of boxers who lived in William Street, at the top of the High Street bank. He was matched with Joe Collins at the Pottery Buildings, a gloomy Victorian Gothic pile in the town's East End. There were men selling oranges and packets of peanuts at the entrance to the hall and my uncle, who was a generous man, bought me some of both. Inside the hall, we moved through a blue haze of cigarette smoke, which made it difficult to see the ring in the centre, and took our seats on the wooden benches.

I was too young to appreciate the finer points of boxing, but it all seemed very exciting to me. There was a lot of shouting by excited spectators and I was impressed by the nobbins - the money thrown into the ring after a good fight. Mickey O'Neill, looking fit and smart in green silk boxing shorts, was top of the bill and my uncle instructed me to shout for him. Unfortunately, Mickey lost on points, which did not please my uncle, nor many others in the hall, for O'Neill was a local favourite who had once been considered as a possible opponent for the great Benny Lynch, although he was now past his prime. I did not realise it at the time but I was witnessing a bit of history: a brief glimpse of the boxing scene of the 1930's. The visit to the boxing match made a deep impression on me and I have been a fight fan ever since.

I have also become interested in the history of boxing on Wearside, which has been largely neglected by historians. Only the late Fred Charlton, a former boxing referee, promoter and matchmaker, has written very much on the subject and this was in the form of a series of articles called 'Round the Rings', which appeared in the *Sunderland Echo* 1955-70. Fred loved the sport and his reminiscences were informative and well written. The paucity of published material prompted me to write *Jack Casey, the Sunderland Assassin* (1991) and the favourable response to its publication has encouraged me to try my hand at a second volume of boxing history, this time covering boxing champions from Wearside.

In a century of boxing history, Wearside has produced six champions, five Northern Area title holders: Jack Casey, Douglas Parker, Roy Mills, Tom Smith and Hughie Smith, and one British and Commonwealth title holder in Billy Hardy. Casey, Parker and Mills started their careers in the 1920's, Parker fighting on into the 1930's, and Casey and Mills into the 1940's. Tom Smith's boxing career began in 1934 and ended in 1947. Hughie Smith had his first professional fight in 1939, picked up what fights he could during the war years, and he took his chance when he got a crack at the Northern Area lightweight title, in 1949. Billy Hardy belongs firmly in the boxing revival of the 1980's.

These six men, then, were Wearside champions, but there could be considerable debate over whether they were Wearside's 'best' boxers. However, it is extremely difficult to define 'best' and to compare the merits of different boxers, especially when they fought in different periods, for boxing, like other sports, has changed over the years. What is beyond dispute is that these six men won titles and other Wearside boxers did not. Perhaps there was an element of good fortune in the winning of their titles, but this is often the case in sport as in other activities. Being the right man in the right place at the right time is often a matter of chance and the margin between success and failure can be very narrow. Therefore, if Wearside boxers, such as Billy Smith, Charlie McDonald, Ginger Rennie, Mickey O'Neill and Bert Ingram are not included here, it is only because they never won a title. Few have ever doubted their fighting qualities. They were, what the Americans call 'nearly men': boxers who, for whatever reasons, did not quite make it into the championship class. Billy Smith was forced to retire at the age of 22, with stomach trouble, just when he had established himself as a leading title contender. Charlie McDonald was handicapped by the colour bar, then in operation in British boxing, and never achieved his full potential. Ginger Rennie lacked a bit of weight, tipping the scales at only 7st 10lb. Mickey O'Neill was unlucky to lose some close decisions and these proved crucial to his championship hopes. Whilst Bert Ingram was only a second away from winning the Northern Area middleweight title, in 1950. Then there were popular Sunderland boxers such as Joe Baldasara, Harry Best, Jack Clansey, Joe Donnelly, Paddy Gill, Wally Knightley, Bob Lamb, Kid Lees, Tommy Oliver, Tom Parker, Private Robson, Paddy Ross, Harry Strongbow, Jim Travers and Danny and Peter Veitch, who topped the bill in ten and fifteen rounders at local stadiums without being considered as title contenders. Up the River Wear, at Durham City, matches were staged in the drill hall and the covered market, and, occasionally, in the open air on the race course. The cathedral city can boast no champions, but it produced some top of the bill performers, such as Mattie Hinds, the pit lad from Belmont.

Some might question Douglas Parker's right to be described as a Wearsider, for, as is well known, he was a Scot, born in Aberdeen, who came to Sunderland as a teenager. However, he settled in the town and he fought and won his Northern Area lightweight title as a resident of Sunderland. He was often described by boxing writers as a Wearside Scot and this seems an appropriate way of describing him. Others might ask why Billy Thompson, the British lightweight champion 1947-51 and European lightweight champion 1948-49 is not included among the Wearside champions. For he was born in New Silksworth, in 1925, and his father took him to watch boxing at Sunderland's

Holmeside Stadium, when he was only four years old.However, Billy's family moved to Yorkshire when he was a young boy and he grew up to consider himself a Yorkshireman. He was always billed as coming from Hickleton Main, near Sheffield. By this line of argument, then, Wearside gains Douglas Parker and loses Billy Thompson.

To get to the top in any sport is a considerable achievement and boxing is a tougher game than most. Few other sports test an individual quite so severely, not only in strength, skill and stamina but also in character, and those who achieve championship status are worthy of respect. This book, then, tells the stories of six Wearsiders who won championships in the ring and sketches the background against which they won their titles.

CHAPTER ONE

BOXING ON WEARSIDE

Boxing activity on Wearside goes back to the bare-knuckle days of the fight game. It is known that the *Lord Byron* tavern, in Maling's Rigg, in Sunderland's East End, was a venue for bare-knuckle bouts, in the 1830's. Contests took place in a large upstairs room, and were promoted by one, George Craggs. A famous visitor to this establishment was James 'Deaf' Burke, the bare-knuckle champion of England, 1833-39.[1] Other Wearside taverns and inns were also probably used as venues for bare-knuckle contests, although few records of such activities have survived. When magistrates began to crack down on prize fighting, in the 1850's and '60's - effectively making it an illegal activity - boxing matches began to be held on remote sites.[2] Fulwell Quarry, Ryhope Dene and a secluded spot at Cleadon were popular venues for bare-knuckle matches, in the area. Contests are also known to have been staged on the cliff tops at Marsden, and at quiet spots along the Sunderland-Hartlepool coast. The longest fight with the bare-knuckles to take place in the area is generally acknowledged to have been fought in 1855, between Dick McKie from Monkwearmouth and Southwick's Tom Johnson, who battled it out over 75 rounds, at Fulwell Dene. This was an eliminating bout, the winner to meet Johnny Robinson of South Shields for the championship of the North. McKie was the lighter of the pair by a stone and, in the end, Johnson's weight advantage gave him the edge over his opponent and McKie retired, a gallant loser. Johnson went on to fight Robinson for £50 a side, the contest being staged in a field near Bishop Auckland. John Robinson was a formidable fighter and he defeated Johnson after 29 gruelling rounds.[3] Another local contest of note was staged at Cleadon, when Paddy McKenna beat Mattie Potts over 20 rounds. A bare-knuckle fight, staged at Ryhope Dene, between

Dick Burge and Bob Forster of Felling, was broken up by the police, causing spectators to scatter in all directions 'except eastwards into the sea'.[4] The fight was resumed at Newcastle, the next day, and was won by Burge, who went on to win the British lightweight championship in 1891, and become famous as a fight promoter at Blackfriars Ring, in London.

With the adoption of the Queensberry Rules, including the use of gloves, plus certain decisions in the courts which no longer held boxing to be illegal, boxing matches ceased to be an underground sporting activity and moved out into the open. In the 1890's, bouts are known to have been staged at the Carpenters' Union Rooms, in Barclay Street, Monkwearmouth, the Golden Lion Hotel in the East End, the Assembly Hall on the corner of Fawcett Street and St Thomas' Street (on the site now occupied by the Midland Bank) and at the Hendon running grounds. The sport always had a popular following in Sunderland and, during the Edwardian period, boxing matches were held at the Skating Rink in Hudson Road, the Star Music Hall in Sans Street, Lambton Club near the Victoria Hall, Felix Scott's fight emporium in High Street East, Will Cameron's boxing pavilion in High Street West and at Frank Guess's big marquee in the Garrison Field.

After the First World War, the Black brothers, George and Alfred, a Wearside family who owned a chain of cinemas in the North East, decided that a town of Sunderland's size and importance, not to mention its boxing tradition, should have a first-class boxing stadium.[5] Accordingly, the Olympia Skating Rink, in Holmeside, was demolished and replaced by the Stadium, a purpose-built, domed boxing arena which seated 3,000 spectators. The farthest seat was only 35 feet from the ring, and the auditorium was arranged in three divisions of outer, middle and inner circles. Inner and middle circle patrons entered by a door in Holmeside and they passed through the Whitehall rink to

The Star Music Hall in Sans Street, one of several pre-1914 boxing venues in Sunderland.

take their seats at the ringside, whilst those who occupied the cheaper seats entered the stadium by a rear door in Park Lane. The stadium had a fully-equipped gymnasium and a shower room for the boxers, and it claimed to be the first boxing arena in the world to provide running water in the boxers' corners. It was a superb boxing stadium of its time and was sometimes referred to as the 'Palace of Punch'.

The management declared that: 'Rowdyism, which is apt to creep into all sports, will not be tolerated',[6] and every effort was made to give the stadium 'class'. For example, the management insisted that all seconds must be 'properly dressed'. Newcastle's Mickey McGuire, then a preliminary fighter who went on to defeat Young Perez, the flyweight champion of the world, recalls how he turned up at the Holmeside Stadium for a fight engagement accompanied by his father, the former boxer Chucky Drane, who was to second him. Mr Drane was wearing a white silk scarf over a collarless shirt - common attire at that time.

> *'Where's your collar and tie?' demanded the doorkeeper.*
>
> *'I always wear this silk scarf.' replied Chucky.*
>
> *'You'll have to go out and buy the needful if you wish to second here,'*

ordered the stadium official, and Chucky Drane had to acquire the appropriate neckwear before he was allowed to enter the dressing rooms.

Alfred Black was managing director of the Holmeside Stadium and Gordon Ray, former welterweight champion of South Africa, was appointed business manager and matchmaker. At the opening of the stadium, Alfred Black announced:

> *'It is the intention of the management to bring some of the very best exponents of the game to the stadium, and if the support is forthcoming to bring the topnotchers, world champions at various weights.'*

The Monkwearmouth Miners' Hall in Roker Avenue which was a venue for boxing throughout the 1930s.

Unfortunately, these ambitions were never realised. The Blacks had conceived their plans for the Holmeside Stadium during the post-war boom, which came to an abrupt end, in 1920. Shipbuilding was particularly hard hit by the recession and unemployment in the town was high throughout the 1920's. The Blacks found it necessary to reduce admission prices and this meant that boxers' purses were low. It was a promoter's market and boxers were grateful for a spot on a boxing bill. Some boxers hung around the doors on fight nights, carrying their kit, in the hope of standing in as a last minute substitute. Nevertheless, the 1920's was the golden age of boxing on Wearside. Sunderland had one of the best stadiums in the country and a plentiful supply of local boxers who drew the crowds. Contests were staged every week and the stadium was usually packed with enthusiastic fight fans.

A host of good local fighters got their chance at the Holmeside Stadium, including Jack Casey, Charlie McDonald, Roy Mills, Douglas Parker and Billy Smith. In spite of paying low wages, the Black brothers always claimed that they never made big profits out of their boxing promotions, and the overhead costs of running a major stadium must have been high. These considerations prompted the Blacks to close the stadium, in June 1930, and to replace it with a large cinema (the *Regal*) and a dancehall (the *Rink*) which proved to be big money spinners over the next thirty years. The Black family were shrewd businessmen.

After the closure of the Holmeside Stadium, small promotions were carried on by George Jackson, and later by Billy Hughes, at the Monkwearmouth Miners' Hall, in Roker Avenue, and continued there until the outbreak of war in 1939. In the summer of 1932, open air matches were staged at Roker Park football stadium and the Fulwell Club grounds. George Jackson, however, was interested in an indoor arena for his promotions and in 1934 he converted the Theatre Royal, in Bedford Street, into a boxing

The old Theatre Royal in Bedford Street which was used as a boxing stadium 1934-36 prior to conversion into a cinema.

stadium.[7] Live theatre at the Royal had been killed off by the advent of the 'talkies' and the building was standing empty when Jackson took it over on a short lease. The new stadium opened with its first bill, on 14 April 1934. The ring was fixed on the stage and spectators had an excellent view from stalls, circle and gallery. The *Royal* had a seating capacity of 2,000 and Jackson knew that admission charges would have to be kept low during a period of depression. Boxers' purses had also improved since the 1920's and, therefore, the wages bill would be higher than it had been for the Black brothers at Holmeside Stadium in the 1920's. George Jackson had few illusions that he had acquired a gold mine, but he had a great love for boxing and also promoted at the Albion Road Stadium, in North Shields. His matchmaker was Jack McBeth, a shipyard plumber by trade, who had boxed professionally in the 1920's, and was a shrewd judge of the fight game. George Jackson was a native of West Hartlepool and he encouraged several fine 'Pools boxers - such as Jack London, George Bunter and Al Capone - to fight at the Royal. Jack Casey, Charlie McDonald and Douglas Parker, then nearing the end of their boxing careers, fought at the Royal, but, perhaps more importantly, the stadium enabled up-and-comers, such as Roy Mills and Tom Smith to fight before their own supporters. The Jackson regime lasted for two years, until the lease came to an end, and the Black family then converted the building into a cinema. The last bill at the Royal was staged on 13 June 1936, when Roy Mills outpointed Bob Simpkins over 15 rounds, in the final eliminator for the Northern Area middleweight title. Fred Charlton, who refereed at the Royal on many occasions, described these as the 'roistering years' and there are still some surviving Wearside fight fans of the 1930's who look back with nostalgia at the splendid bouts they saw there.

Billy Hughes took over the small promotions at the Monkwearmouth Miners' Hall. Billy Hughes was one of boxing's most colourful characters. He came from Seaham and, in his

The Pottery Buildings in Sunderland's East End where boxing matches were staged 1938-40.

younger days, he had been a British Army champion and a Pitman's Champion, and had once gone sixteen rounds with Digger Stanley, the World and British bantamweight champion, 1910-13. As a part-time occupation, he often assisted Albert Pierrepoint, the hangman, in carrying out executions at Durham Gaol. In the 1930's, Hughes had turned promoter and he put on open-air fights at the Culture Grounds, in Seaham, as well as promoting fights in Sunderland. The Monkwearmouth Miners' Hall was hard pressed to hold 500 people and the revenue barely covered the costs Billy Hughes incurred in putting on the shows, but Billy was content to be involved in the fight game and he persuaded Jack Casey, Roy Mills and Tom Smith, among others, to box there for small purses.

Meanwhile, George Jackson looked for a larger stadium in the town. He tried to secure the Victoria Hall for matches, which could seat 2,000 people, and it would have been an ideal venue for boxing in terms of its size, facilities and central location. It had been used for the staging of amateur boxing contests, but its owner, the Sunderland Town Council, was not prepared to extend this to professional boxing. Instead, the Council offered Mr Jackson the use of the Pottery Buildings and he staged his first promotion there in September 1938. The Pottery Buildings were located in the docks area of the town and its hall could only accommodate 800 spectators, ruling out major promotions. Attendances at Jackson's first fight nights were only modest, although numbers picked up over the following months and boxing continued to be staged there until June 1940. Hughie Smith, a future Northern Area lightweight champion, made his professional debut at the Pottery Buildings, in October 1939.

In April 1940, George Jackson promoted the biggest boxing event seen on Wearside since the closure of the Holmeside Stadium, ten years before. The Victoria Hall was the venue for a boxing tournament held in aid of the Mayor's Forces Fund. In a top of

Open air boxing at Roker Park football ground: referee Tommy Watson gives his pre-fight instructions to Hughie Smith and Ted Duffy, 4 August 1945.

the bill contest, Sunderland's Tom Smith, Northern Area featherweight champion, defeated Jim Keery of Lisburn, a leading contender for the Irish title; and, in a supporting bout, Hughie Smith outpointed Jackie 'Kid' Horseman of West Hartlepool. Seat prices were 3/6d, 2/- and 1/- and the promotion was a complete sell-out, with many people being turned away at the doors. The Town Council had always been reluctant to allow the august Victoria Hall to be used for professional boxing matches and had only given way on this occasion in support of a good cause. The aldermen and councillors, who attended the charity boxing evening, said afterwards that they had been impressed by the good behaviour of the crowd and would be prepared to consider further promotions at this venue. Unfortunately, a year later, the ill-fated Victoria Hall was demolished by a German parachute mine and in May 1943 the Pottery Buildings were severely damaged in an air-raid, leaving Sunderland without a suitable large hall for boxing contests.

Boxing on Wearside was kept alive in the 1940's mainly by the efforts of promoter, Fred Simm.[8] Simm was a lifelong boxing supporter who had seen something of fight promotion when he held the catering concession at the Royal stadium, in the 1930's. During the Second World War, he promoted a series of boxing programmes in aid of charity. In April 1943, he used the Seaburn Hall to raise money for the Red Cross, and followed this up by staging open air contests at Ashbrooke cricket ground and Roker Park football stadium, as part of Sunderland's Holidays at Home programme. The wartime public was starved of entertainment and Simm's promotion, at Roker Park in August 1945, drew a crowd of 8,000, the biggest attendance at a boxing match in Sunderland's history. The crowd saw Tom Smith outpoint Kid Tanner of British Guiana over ten rounds, and in a supporting bout, Hughie Smith knocked out Bradford's Ted Duffy, in the second of an eight round contest.

Fred Simm, the promoter who kept boxing alive on Wearside in the 1940s.

After the war, Simm began promoting on his own account, first at Horden, then, more successfully, at Darlington, with local light heavyweight and future Northern Area champion, Dave Davis, pulling in the crowds. In 1948, Simm opened the Ryhope Arena, converting the grounds of Ryhope Hall into an open air stadium. It was an attractive setting for boxing, reminiscent in some ways of the open-air bare-knuckle contests which had been staged at the nearby Ryhope Dene, in the 19th century. The stadium was only a short bus ride from the Sunderland town centre and the site was extremely convenient for boxing fans travelling from the surrounding colliery villages. Terry Cullen, Gene Devlin, Bob Hodgson and Bert Ingram were popular local performers on Simm's bills.

Britain's post-war boxing boom was well underway and, in May 1949, Simm extended his open-air promotions to the Hendon cricket ground, in Sunderland. It was here, on 17 August 1949, that Sunderland's Hughie Smith outpointed Jimmy Trotter of Shildon for the Northern Area lightweight title. In the summer of 1952, Fred Simm switched his promotions to an open-air site at Park Lane in the centre of Sunderland. His first promotions were a sell-out but bad weather rained off some subsequent bills - always a hazard with open-air promotions - and, when his lease on the site ended, in 1953, Simm retired as a promoter and became the agent for a furniture firm.

Boxing on Wearside then entered the doldrums. Britain's post-war boxing boom was coming to an end. The doubling of entertainment tax in the 1953 budget, squeezed many small promoters out of business, and the lack of a suitable indoor stadium handicapped promotions in the Sunderland area. Wearside boxers had to travel farther afield in search of matches, but, in any case, there were fewer young men entering the sport. Full employment, rising living standards and alternative forms of entertainment no doubt played their part in this trend. Boxing

Hendon Cricket Ground where open air boxing was staged 1949-52.

appeared to be a dying sport on Wearside, and even New St James Hall in nearby Newcastle went over to bingo in 1968.

The North East's boxing revival in the 1980's, owed much to the efforts of John Spensely.[9] Spensely was a former heavyweight boxer from Middlesbrough who had built up a successful radio-taxi and hire-car business on Teesside. He began by providing training facilities for local lads and discovered that there were still young men keen to take up the sport, but there was nowhere for them to fight. In May 1977, with Tommy Miller as matchmaker, he promoted a dinner and boxing evening at the Marton Country Club in Cleveland. The show was a complete sell-out and he followed it up with other successful promotions in the area. In March 1978, he brought topline boxing back to Sunderland with a show at the Mecca Centre. Spensely showed that there was a demand for professional boxing shows in the area and the opening of big leisure centres provided the modern stadiums the sport had previously lacked. He led where other promoters have followed.

Sunderland's Crowtree Leisure Centre proved to be a good venue for boxing promotions, and Frank and Brian Deans promoted the first boxing show there in June 1987. Five months later, the same venue was used by the same promoters to stage a British and Commonwealth heavyweight title fight between Birmingham's Horace Notice and Paul Lister from Newcastle. Local fighter, Billy Hardy, defended his British bantamweight title there, in 1988 and 1989, and, in January 1990, he met Orlando Canizales in a challenge for the IBF World bantamweight title.

Modern stadiums would have been of little use, however, unless there had been a supply of fighters prepared to step into the ring, and the 1980's saw the emergence of a new generation of local boxers eager for success. Billy Hardy came up through boys' club boxing and his success in the ring, winning British and Commonwealth titles, has made him a local hero. Glenn

Three featherweight champions in the ring:
John Davison (British titleholder) Billy Hardy (Commonwealth) and Frank Foster (Northern Area) at Annette Conroy's promotion, Gateshead, 23 October 1992

Tommy Conroy's gym on the banks of the River Wear

McCrory, born in Stanley in 1964 fought as an amateur for Consett Sports Club and, after turning professional, in 1984, he became the first fighter from the North East to win a world title when he defeated Patrick Lumumba on points over 12 rounds , to gain the vacant IBF cruiserweight championship. In March 1993, the immensely popular Glenn opened the Victoria boxing gym in Felling where he intends to train for his fights and to help develop local boxing talent.

Tommy Conroy, a Sunderland newsagent with a fine record as an amateur boxer, began to train local fighters, in the 1980's, and he is now at the heart of the Tyne and Wear boxing revival.[10] He built a gymnasium at the rear of his newsagent's shop in High Street East and his stable of fighters includes top British featherweight fighter, John Davison. Tommy Conroy's wife, Annette, is the North East's first female promoter. Tommy trains and manages the boxers and Annette organises the fight nights. They make a good team and are well known figures in the North East's boxing scene of the 1990's. After successful promotions at the Gateshead Leisure Centre, the Conroys teamed up with Glasgow promoter, Tommy Gilmour, to promote the John Davison - Tim Driscoll contest for the British featherweight title, at the Crowtree Leisure Centre on 10 September 1992, and the John Davison - Steve Robinson bout for the vacant WBO World featherweight championship at the Northumbria Centre, Washington, on 17 April 1993.

No account of the boxing scene, on Wearside, would be complete without a mention of the Sunderland and District Ex-Boxers' Association (SEBA). The Association was founded in 1959, and its first chairman was Jack Wharton, a licensed bookmaker who had boxed professionally in the 1930's. SEBA meets monthly at the Hendon Gardens Hotel. This public house is managed by John Brown, a good amateur boxer in his day, who has covered the walls of his pub with old boxing photographs and posters. SEBA's

Tommy Conroy, manager and trainer, with
Annette Conroy the North East's first
lady promoter.

president is Bert Ingram, who fought for the Northern Area middleweight title in 1950. The Association helps to keep ex-boxers in touch with each other, it organises social evenings and amateur boxing contests, and it distributes a monthly newsletter to members.

Billy Charlton and Tom Smith at Ex-Boxers' Association social evening.

CHAPTER TWO

JACK CASEY

Northern Area Middleweight Champion 1932-34

Jack Casey, widely known as 'Cast iron' Casey because of his toughness, was never knocked out in 224 fights, in a boxing career stretching from 1926 to 1942. He was stopped nine times within the distance, seven times with cuts or a damaged ear and, in two cases, the referee intervened to save him from taking further punishment, but Casey never had the dreaded ten counted over him as he lay on the canvas. It was said of 19th century Sunderland that it was a town where wooden ships were built by iron men - well, Casey was certainly true to the town's tradition: he was the iron man of British boxing. He won the Northern Area middleweight title, in 1932 but failed to defeat Len Harvey when he fought him for the British title later in the same year. He was a shade unlucky not to be given a shot at the British cruiserweight championship in 1934, when Tommy Farr was chosen to meet Eddie Phillips for the vacant title. Yet, Casey's fame rests more on the strength of his jaw than on the winning of titles, although he was always something more than a human punch-bag, for he packed a good punch and had great strength and stamina.[1]

Jack Casey was born on 22 September 1908, in the Southwick area of the town, but his parents, John and Elizabeth, moved to the East End shortly after his birth.[2] Jack's father was a ship riveter by trade. Jack attended the Gray School, where he was an average pupil in most respects except that he excelled at sport and captained the school's football team.

After Jack left school, he worked as a newspaper boy and became a professional boxer by chance. He was a regular attender at the Holmeside Stadium and was there on 17 July 1926 when one of

JACK CASEY

the contestants in a novices' flyweight competition withdrew. Seventeen year old Casey was drafted in as a last minute replacement. He knocked out one W.Teasdale in the first round of his heat and, in the final, boxed a four round draw with Jim Britton. That night, Alfred Black wrote in his stadium diary: 'Casey looks good'.

Casey joined Duggie Morton's school of boxing and trained in the evenings, after he had sold his newspapers. Jack's father had done some boxing as a young man and he encouraged his son to take up the game. On 6 November 1926, Jack Casey entered another novices' competition, at the Holmeside Stadium, when he lost to Jim Britton in the first heat. In spite of this defeat, Duggie Morton considered he was ready to move out of the novices' class and Casey was matched with George Willis in a six rounds contest, at North Shields. The match was a slug feast and the referee declared it a draw. In a rematch, a fortnight later, Jack Casey won a decisive points victory over the Tyne Dock fighter.

Jack Casey was kept busy in 1927: he fought 30 times and won 22 of his bouts. He had not yet developed his crouching style and still fought in the traditional English way, although it was clear even then that he was very tough. On 4 November 1927, he was stopped for the first time in his boxing career by Peel Bell. The Carlisle fighter caught Casey with a hard right on the ear and the referee persuaded Casey to retire to have this examined by the doctor. Three fights later, against Pat Crawford, he again had to retire with ear trouble.

In the summer of 1928, Casey did some campaigning in Lancashire rings and began to get himself known outside North East England. On 9 December 1928, he met the Anglo-Italian boxer, Dino Guselli, who Casey claimed was his hardest opponent up to that time. Guselli hit him with everything he had but Casey refused to go down and he claimed that this was the first time he had realised the strength of his jaw. After the fight, the Royton promoter, Joe Tolley, said: '*Where did you get that cast-iron jaw, Casey?*' And the name stuck.

In 1929, Casey was fighting 12 and 15 rounders as a welter weight and his distinctive style was beginning to emerge. He was so tough he did not need to worry too much about defence, leaning forward in a crouch with his hands held low, he would take blows to the face without flinching, ready to leap in with his own punches. Casey liked nothing better than to slug it out, and few were better at wearing an opponent down, however he was less successful against accomplished boxers, as his record shows. In 1929, he was beaten four times by Albert Johnson, a black fighter from Manchester and brother of the more famous Len.[3] Johnson was tall with a fast left jab and forced Casey's retirement on two occasions, in 1929. Another boxer with a good straight left was Jack Harbin, a miner from Usworth, who defeated Casey twice on points in 1929,[4] and George Willis from Newcastle, another left hand artist, who notched up two victories over Casey, in the same year.[5] Casey's rise to prominence was not meteoric, he learned his trade the hard way.

During the course of 1930, Casey moved up into the middleweight class and over the year he marked up 25 wins against 9 losses with one drawn bout. He lost decisions to Archie Sexton, Sandy McKenzie, Charlie McDonald, Joe Lowther and Harry Mason, but it was no disgrace to lose to men of this calibre. They were all skilful boxers who could hold Casey off and pile up the points with a good left jab. Casey's and Sexton's paths were to cross five times in their ring careers and on this, their first meeting, Sexton ran out, a comfortable winner on points over 15 rounds. Casey fought Sandy McKenzie twice, in 1930, the second time on a special bill to mark the opening of New St James Hall in Newcastle on 12 May 1930, and Casey met Charlie McDonald, a fortnight later, to mark the closing of the

Holmeside Stadium in Sunderland, on 31 May 1930.

Casey v McDonald looked an inspired match, for here were two of Wearside's most popular fighters meeting in the ring for the first time, and both men had their supporters among local fight fans.[6] Yet the match failed to produce the expected fireworks. Both men knew each other too well and this made for a dull fight, which McDonald won on points. Joe Lowther won the Northern Area middleweight title in 1930 and he fought Casey five times, in the same year. Lowther won three of the contests and Casey two. In the fourth fight, Lowther forced Casey to retire in the eleventh round with a badly cut face, becoming one of the eight men who managed to stop the cast-iron man inside the distance. Harry Mason, the former British lightweight champion was a crafty boxer who outpointed Casey over 12 rounds at Leeds. Among Casey's wins in 1930, was a victory over Sonny Bird, a clever London fighter.

1931 was the year when Jack Casey made the breakthrough into big time boxing. He started the year with wins over Joe Woodruff and Archie Sexton and then lost four consecutive fights, but he went on to win his next 14 fights, 10 of them inside the distance, and it was at this time that Jack Smith, the Lancashire promoter dubbed him the 'Sunderland Assassin', a cognomen which stuck to him for the remainder of his boxing career. This string of victories and his growing reputation for toughness brought Casey to the attention of London promoter, Jeff Dickson.

Dickson was lining up an Anglo-French boxing bill, at the Royal Albert Hall, and he was looking for someone prepared to enter the ring against the redoubtable French middleweight champion, Marcel Thil. Thil was a future world champion and he had already beaten the British middleweight champion, Len Harvey, and the British welterweight champion, Jack Hood. Few British fighters were keen to climb into the ring with Thil and the

New St James Hall in Gallowgate, Newcastle, known as the 'graveyard of champions'. It was the premier boxing stadium in North East England 1930-68.

fight was offered to Casey for a purse of £50. Casey accepted the offer and paid his first visit to London. Rather foolishly, he spent the day of the fight looking at the sights, when he would have benefited from a rest on the afternoon of the contest. Casey, however, was never overawed by an opponent and he gave a good account of himself that night. He caused a minor sensation in the opening round when he split Thil's left eyebrow with a fierce right hand punch. The eye bled for five rounds and there was a strong possibility that the Frenchman might be forced to retire. A ripple of excitement ran through the crowd who sensed the possibility of an upset, but Thil's handlers did a good bit of patching up on the cut, and Thil began to treat Casey with more respect. In the sixth round, Thil, aware that his cut eye made him vulnerable, went all out to finish the fight with a knock-out, but in doing so he left himself open to another of Casey's right hand smashes. Over the last four rounds, Thil hammered his way to a points victory. Next day, the national newspapers were full of praise for Casey's courageous performance.[7]

Jack Casey entered 1932 at the peak of his fighting form. Walter Russell had taken over as his manager and his aim was to get Casey a British title fight. John Paget, the New St James Hall promoter, had secured Len Harvey's agreement to fight Casey in Newcastle, but the Board of Control refused to sanction the match as a championship bout. The fight went ahead as a 15 round non-title match, on 8 February 1932.

Casey took the fight to Harvey from the opening bell, forcing the champion onto the defensive. In round 4, Harvey caught Casey with one of his best combinations: a left hook to the body followed by a right to the jaw. The punches put Casey on the canvas but he was up immediately and continued to stalk the champion. After the failure to deliver a knock-out, Harvey resorted to 'spoiling', smothering Casey's attacks and countering with a left jab, until the last two rounds, when he went on the attack again. Harvey had done enough to win and was awarded the decision on points.

After Jock McAvoy had been defeated by Len Harvey in his bid for the British middleweight title, on 21 March 1932, the Board of Control ruled that the Rochdale Thunderbolt must defend his Northern Area title against Jack Casey, and the fight took place at Manchester, on 18 July 1932. Jock McAvoy was an aggressive two-handed fighter with a string of knock-outs to his credit, but he chose to follow hit and run tactics against Casey. Jack Casey moved relentlessly forward in his usual style and McAvoy was content to keep the fight at long range and pile up the points. McAvoy appeared to be coasting to an easy points victory until the eleventh round, when Casey caught him with a left hook that sent McAvoy's gum-shield spinning across the ring. Casey continued to bore in during the twelfth round and there were some fierce exchanges as McAvoy reverted to his normal aggressive style. This suited Casey and, in round thirteen, he rocked McAvoy with a vicious uppercut. The fourteenth proved to be the last round. McAvoy switched his attacks to the body and put Casey on the canvas with a left hook. There was an appeal for a foul from Casey's corner but the referee, Tom Gamble, ignored it. Casey rose and McAvoy, believing he had found Casey's weak spot, launched another barrage of body punches. Casey went down and lay writhing in agony on the canvas but this time the referee ordered McAvoy back to his corner and awarded the decision to Casey on a disqualification.[8] Casey's supporters had arranged for a brass band to greet him on his arrival at Sunderland railway station, but when Casey learned of this, he got off the train at West Hartlepool and travelled home by road to avoid the welcome planned for him.

After his defeat of McAvoy, the Board of Control ruled that Casey should meet Archie Sexton in a final eliminator for Harvey's British middleweight title. The fight took place at New

St James Hall, on 3 October 1932. Both men boxed cautiously for the first six rounds, then, in round seven, Casey launched a whirlwind of punches at Sexton: a left jab to the nose was followed by a right to Sexton's temple and a left hook to the jaw. Sexton went down and was counted out holding his right glove over his eyes. Few could deny that Casey had earned his crack at the British title.

The fight took place at New St James Hall, on 12 December 1932.[9] The referee made it clear to Len Harvey early in the fight that he would not tolerate excessive holding. Casey forced the pace from the opening bell, although he did not bore in on Harvey in his usual style. The first five rounds were fairly even, then in the sixth round, Casey caught Harvey with a hard right to the jaw. Harvey fell back on the ropes with his arms dangling by his sides. The champion looked to be out on his feet and it appeared that it needed only one good punch to finish him off but Casey, fearing a trick, hesitated, giving Harvey vital seconds to clear his head and slide off the ropes. After the fight, Harvey admitted that he had been in trouble at this point. The sixth round was a bad one for Harvey in another respect: he cracked his right hand on Casey's jaw and had to nurse it for the remainder of the fight. Casey's aggression won him the middle rounds but Harvey began to look stronger in the ninth, tenth and eleventh rounds, then, halfway through the twelfth round, Casey caught the champion with another right, flush on the jaw, which sent him staggering back on the ropes. As in the sixth round, Casey held off, allowing Harvey time to recover. Harvey was always a strong finisher and he won the last four rounds, ending with a grandstand finish in the fifteenth round. The referee awarded the decision to Harvey who retained the Lonsdale Belt. After his retirement from the ring, Harvey nominated this as the hardest fight of his career. Casey had come very close to winning the title.

The Harvey fight put Casey at the peak of his boxing career and promoters were keen to have such a colourful fighter on their bills. There were several options open to the cast-iron man. Casey wanted a return bout with Harvey, although he conceded that he would probably have to fight an eliminating contest with Jock McAvoy before he got another crack at the middleweight title. There were also negotiations underway which would match Casey with Marcel Thil for the world middleweight championship. Although Casey was not the British champion, there was nothing to stop such a fight taking place and promoters knew that it would draw the crowds. Casey was also in touch with Charlie Harvey who handled the contracts for British boxers fighting in the United States. The Americans were very keen to see Casey in action in their rings and Harvey was confident he could line up a number of lucrative contracts. After his title fight, Casey said he would wait to see what came of the negotiations for a fight with Thil, then, in March 1933, he hoped to go to America for a few fights, and by the time he returned from the States, the position concerning the British middleweight championship should have been sorted out by the Board of Control, and Casey was confident he would be involved in their plans. Casey was also the Northern Area middleweight champion and he could expect to be defending his title in 1933.

In the event, none of these things happened. There was no return contest with Thil: the Frenchman defended his world title against Kid Tunero, in 1933. The negotiations for a trip to the U.S.A. were unsuccessful: the depression was squeezing American promoters and Casey could not be guaranteed a series of fights in American rings. McAvoy was given the next championship fight with Len Harvey and Jack Casey did not defend his Northern Area title. Several promoters were interested in matching Casey with Tommy Moore for the Northern title but the Board of Control withheld its approval and the fight never took place.

Instead, Jack Casey chose to fight every fortnight against anyone the promoters lined up for him, and his opponents included the South African middleweight champion, Eddie McGuire; the Australian light heavyweight champion, Leo Bandias; and the leading British middleweight title contender, Archie Sexton. On 24 May 1933, he fought Carmelo Candel, in Paris. Casey travelled to France with a big reputation as the man who had nearly defeated Marcel Thil. The French fans, however, were disappointed by his performance against Candel. A jaded Casey had little to offer except his toughness and he retired at the end of the fifth round with a battered face and a badly cut eye. A fortnight later, looking more like the Assassin of old, he finished off Dino Guselli in two rounds, and ten days after this he stepped into the ring with Jack London, in an open air contest at the Engineers' Club in West Hartlepool.

Jack London - a future British and Empire heavyweight champion - was then an up-and-coming heavyweight of twenty years of age. He was young but no novice with 41 fights under his belt. Casey weighed in at 12 stone, conceding two stones plus height and reach to London, who was a fully fledged heavyweight.

The promoters knew that the fight would be a sell-out. Jack London was a local lad and Casey had been a popular performer in Hartlepool rings over the years. A win over Jack Casey would look good in London's record: but what did Casey hope to gain by agreeing to the match? Apparently, it was money. Casey was planning a Mediterranean cruise in the summer and was tempted by the big purse offer.

The fight took place in pouring rain, although the capacity crowd of three thousand sat it out to the last punch. Casey opened in whirlwind fashion, going for a quick knock-out, but London survived these early attacks and thereafter it was Jack London all the way. He dropped Casey to the canvas in the fourth round, although he bounced up straight away and never stopped throwing punches, but when Casey hit the deck again, in the tenth round, many in the crowd began to wonder if they were about to witness Casey being counted out for the first time in his ring career. Then, in the interval between rounds ten and eleven, London announced his retirement due to a damaged right hand. It was a sensational end to the fight and most spectators were astounded at this turn of events. Some criticised London's decision to withdraw when he was so far ahead on points and with Casey looking well beaten, but there were still five rounds to go and London felt he could not face Casey with an injured right hand. The decision, therefore, went to Jack Casey and he had his iron jaw to thank for the victory.

In October 1933, Casey started a sequence of 12 wins and one drawn bout, including victories over Paul Schaefer, Bushman Dempster, Reggie Meen, Charlie Belanger, Tommy Farr and George Slack. Meen was a former British heavyweight champion, Belanger held the Canadian light heavyweight title, Tommy Farr, the Welsh light heavyweight title, and George Slack was the Northern Area heavyweight champion.[10] In March 1934, Casey relinquished his Northern Area middleweight title on the grounds that he could no longer make the 11 st. 6lbs limit and he seemed more comfortable campaigning as a cruiserweight, as the results show. His victory over Tommy Farr, on 23 April 1934, was one of the most impressive of his career. The two men, both tough and ringwise, fought it out over 12 gruelling rounds and there is little doubt that Casey deserved the decision. Casey, therefore, could consider himself unlucky when Tommy Farr was matched with Eddie Phillips for the vacant British light heavyweight title, in February 1935.

However, Casey carried on, meeting heavyweights such as Erich Seelig, Manuel Abrew and Ginger Hauxwell, as well as light heavyweights like Leonard Steyaert, the Belgian champion, and American, Jimmy Tarante.

The top cruiserweights of 1934.

In January 1935, Casey tackled Charlie Smith, the giant from Deptford. Casey put him down for a count of nine in the third round, but the Wearsider was forced to retire with a badly cut eye in the seventh round. Casey's next fight was against the German, Helmuth Hartkopp. Casey put the German on the canvas for a count of nine in the first round, but Hartkopp, like Smith, was too big and strong for Casey and the German took the decision on points.

These two punishing defeats at the hands of heavyweights should have shown Casey the folly of taking on men from the heavier division, but then Casey was tempted by a good offer from Jack McBeth, matchmaker at the Royal Stadium, in Sunderland. Would Casey be interested in a return match with Jack London? The money was right so Casey agreed to meet the West Hartlepool heavyweight for a second time.

Jack London had improved since their last meeting, two years before, whereas Casey was now past his prime. London was in top form and he held a two stone advantage over Casey. As always, Casey was game but London was well ahead over the twelve rounds.

Casey retired after this fight and became the manager of Polly's Tavern, in Lambton Street. The pub did good business and Casey was a popular host, but he proved to be a soft touch as a publican: too many drinks were chalked up on the slate and never paid for and too many free rounds were given. Casey lost money running the pub and twenty months later he returned to the ring.

Jack Casey was twenty-nine years old when he made his comeback. Not very old as boxers go, but few boxers had soaked up as much punishment and his style of fighting relied on strength and aggression. Did he still have it in him? "They never come back" is an old saying in the fight game and there are few exceptions to the general rule. Jack Casey was not one of them.

The first fight in his comeback campaign was against Jackie Moran, at New St James Hall, on 6 December 1937. Moran was a young light heavyweight from Carlisle who worked as an engine driver on the LMS. The match was intended to serve as a warm-up fight for Casey, but it did not turn out that way. Casey weighed in at 13st 1lb, a stone above his pre-retirement weight and, although he was as tough and game as ever, his old snap was missing. Moran kept the fight at long range with his left jab and he emerged a comfortable winner on points over the ten rounds.

A fortnight later, Casey faced Reggie Meen at the same venue and he stopped the former British heavyweight champion in the second round. Three weeks after this, Casey beat Ron Linley at Bournemouth, the referee stopping the contest in the fifth round, and this proved to be the last win of Casey's boxing career. He had four more fights that year, against up-and-coming heavyweights, and lost them all. Casey lost on points over ten rounds to Stan Kirby, at Darlington; to Jim McKenzie over ten rounds, at Newcastle; to Zachy Nicholas over ten rounds, at Penzance; and on 6 April 1938, Casey was forced to retire in the third round against Canadian fighter, Packy Paul, at Sheffield. He then hung up his gloves for a second time.

Casey worked as a labourer on building sites until the outbreak of war in 1939, when he enlisted in the King's Own Scottish Borderers. He performed a variety of duties during his time in the Army: he was a physical training instructor, a guard at a POW camp and served as a lance corporal in the Garrison Military Police. He had a few matches in Army boxing competitions and in 1942, he fought his last professional contest. On 22 February 1942, he faced a young Irish heavyweight, Martin Thornton, at Loughborough. Thornton, known as the 'Connemara Crusher', was being groomed for the Irish heavyweight championship.[11] It had been four years since Casey had last fought professionally: he was ring-rusty, overweight - tipping the scales at 14st 2lbs - and under trained. The hard-hitting Thornton pounded Casey with his haymakers until the sixth round when the referee stepped in to halt the contest. It was after this fight that Casey began to suffer headaches and blackouts, and he was remustered to the Pioneer Corps. He was posted to Cardiff, where he operated the smoke screens used to protect the docks during air-raids. In 1944, he was invalided out of the Army.

After leaving the Army, Jack Casey had a number of labouring jobs, but, in the 1950's, his health deteriorated so much he could no longer hold down a job, and his last years were a constant battle against ill health. He was a member of the Sunderland Ex-Boxers' Association and enjoyed an occasional trip to the boxers' reunions in London. Len Harvey never lost touch with him, and Archie Sexton's son, Dave, always sought him out when he brought his team to play at Roker Park . Jack's devoted wife, Elizabeth, died in 1976, and he died in hospital on 24 January 1980. A service was held for him at Sunderland Parish Church and he was buried in Sunderland Cemetery.

THE STADIUM
SATURDAY, FEBRUARY 22nd.
15-Rounds Contest.—
JACK CASEY
(Sunderland) v.
SONNY BIRD
(London).
TOMMY MASON v. KELLY SHANKS.
KID ENWRIGHT v. DAN TOKELL.
Other Bouts.
POPULAR PRICES: 6d. 1/6, and 2/4.
FEB. 26:—NOVICES' NIGHT. Entries Wanted.

NEW ST. JAMES'S HALL
7.30——TO-NIGHT——7.30.
JACK LORD V. JACK CLANSEY.
PRICES:, 1s., 1s. 10d., 2s. 6d.
MONDAY NIGHT, OCTOBER 3rd.
JACK CASEY, SUNDERLAND.
ARCHIE SEXTON, LONDON.
ACCOMMODATION 5,000.
GOOD SEATS STILL AVAILABLE.
FOR THE BEST FIGHT OF THE SEASON
DON'T BE DISAPPOINTED. BOOK NOW.
6s., 4s. (Bookable), 2s. 6d., 1s. 3d.

BOXING! Phone 2552
ROYAL STADIUM, SUNDERLAND
SATURDAY—7.30
Great Twelve Three-Minute Rounds
JACK CASEY v. JACK LONDON
(Sunderland) (Hartlepool)
Both Men Appear at Two o'clock
TEN ROUNDS
KID DONALD v. KID DOYLE
(Houghton) (Middlesbrough)
SEAMAN WILLIAMS v. KID McCAULEY
(Sunderland) (Middlesbrough)
OTHER CONTESTS
PRICES: 1/-, 2/-, 3/- (Bookable).
Cheap Excursion Tickets from:
Hartlepool, Horden, and Murton

JACK CASEY'S RING RECORD 1926-42

1926			
17 Jul	W Teasdale	w ko 1	Sunderland
17 Jul	Jim Britton	drew 4	Sunderland
6 Nov	Jim Britton	l pts 6	Sunderland
20 Dec	George Willis	drew 6	North Shields
1927			
8 Jan	George Willis	w pts 6	Jarrow
17 Jan	Young Scott	w pts 6	Hetton-le-Hole
29 Jan	Teddy Welsh	l pts 6	South Shields
7 Feb	Alf Bainbridge	l pts 6	North Shields
19 Mar	Eddie McGurk	drew 6	Tyne Dock
28 Mar	Eddie McGurk	l pts 6	Tyne Dock
2 Apr	Alf Smith	w ret 4	North Shields
16 Apr	Joe Kennedy	w pts 6	Tyne Dock
30 Apr	Eddie McGurk	w pts 6	Sunderland
16 May	Teddy Welsh	w pts 6	Newcastle
21 May	Owen McIvor	w ret 4	Sunderland
4 Jun	Jim Britton	w pts 6	Washington
11 Jun	Jim Britton	drew 6	Sunderland
18 Jun	Barney Ward	w ko 3	Tyne Dock
2 Jul	Slogger Bingham	w pts 6	Tyne Dock

6 Aug	Jack Graham	w pts 10	Tyne Dock
29 Aug	Phil Guerin	w ret 3	Newcastle
10 Sep	Owen McIvor	w ko 2	Sunderland
17 Sep	Tommy East	w rsc 5	Newcastle
24 Sep	Danny Veitch	w pts 10	Sunderland
1 Oct	Young Josephs	w rsc 7	Newcastle
8 Oct	Joe Woodie	w pts 6	Sunderland
10 Oct	Joe Kennedy	w rsc 6	Tyne Dock
24 Oct	Pat Crawford	w ret 8	Newcastle
4 Nov	Peel Bell	l ret 8	Carlisle
12 Nov	Bob Phillips	w pts 10	Sunderland
3 Dec	Bob Phillips	w pts 10	Newcastle
12 Dec	Pat Crawford	l ret 4	Newcastle
17 Dec	Dave Dowd	w pts 10	Sunderland
26 Dec	Jim Birch	l pts 10	Leeds
1928			
14 Jan	Con Tansey	w ret 7	Sunderland
21 Jan	Young Giffo	w rsc 7	Sunderland
30 Jan	Pat Crawford	w dis 5	Newcastle
20 Feb	Tommy Woods	drew 10	Tyne Dock
4 Mar	Billy Mack	w pts 10	Leeds
10 Mar	Jack Turner	l pts 10	Sunderland

17 Mar	Andy Keating	w pts 10	Tyne Dock
14 Apr	Joe Grewer	w pts 10	Sunderland
2 Jun	Terry Donlon	w ret 7	Ashton under Lyme
16 Jun	Stan Bradbury	w pts 10	Ashton under Lyme
8 Jul	Al Kenny	drew 15	Salford
20 Jul	Charlie Dickenson	l pts 15	Openshaw
7 Aug	Jim Harrison	w ko 3	Ashton under Lyme
19 Aug	Jock McFarlane	w pts 15	Royton
24 Aug	Jack Hines	l pts 15	Openshaw
1 Sep	Joe Grewer	w ret 7	Sunderland
29 Sep	Charlie Dickenson	w ret 7	Sunderland
5 Oct	Young Giffo	l pts 15	Newcastle
27 Oct	Paul McGuire	w pts 12	Sunderland
4 Nov	Lion Smith	w rsc 1	Leeds
13 Nov	Peter Bottomley	w pts 10	Edinburgh
18 Nov	Ernest Kaye	w pts 12	Leeds
23 Nov	Charlie Lee	w rsc 3	Darlington
1 Dec	Ted Abbott	w pts 15	Sunderland
7 Dec	Alec Law	w dis 6	Darlington
9 Dec	Dino Guselli	w pts 15	Royton

16 Dec	Ernest Kaye	w pts 12	Leeds
21 Dec	Ernest Kaye	drew 12	Hartlepool
1929			
12 Jan	Jack Harbin	l pts 12	Sunderland
21 Jan	Willie Upton	l pts 12	Edinburgh
27 Jan	Fred Oldfield	w pts 12	Leeds
8 Feb	Ted Abbott	drew 15	Darlington
16 Feb	Peter Kelly	w pts 12	Sunderland
22 Feb	Ted Abbott	drew 12	Darlington
24 Feb	Tom Gregson	w rsc 8	Leeds
2 Mar	Jack Harbin	l pts 12	Newcastle
11 Mar	Bob Cockburn	w pts 12	Edinburgh
18 Mar	Ted Abbott	w pts 15	South Shields
23 Mar	Franz Kruppel	l pts 15	Sunderland
20 Apr	Jack Marshall	w pts 15	Sunderland
28 Apr	Seaman Smart	w ret 6	Leeds
19 May	Pat O'Brien	l pts 15	Leeds
25 May	Franz Kruppel	w pts 15	Sunderland
6 Jun	Albert Johnson	l ret 7	Sunderland
16 Jun	Albert Johnson	l pts 12	Leeds
29 Jun	Fred Oldfield	l pts 15	Sunderland
2 Aug	Albert Johnson	l pts 15	Middlesbrough

24 Aug	George Willis	l pts 15	Sunderland
25 Aug	Alec Thake	w pts 15	Leeds
21 Sep	George Willis	l pts 15	Sunderland
4 Oct	Ted Robinson	drew 12	Preston
19 Oct	Albert Johnson	l rsc 6	Sunderland
25 Oct	Ted Robinson	w pts 12	Preston
2 Nov	Mick Harris	w ko 6	Sunderland
9 Nov	Fred Oldfield	drew 15	Hartlepool
9 Dec	Joe Woodruff	l pts 15	Hartlepool
27 Dec	Jim Pearson	w ret 8	Preston
30 Dec	Fred Oldfield	w pts 15	Hartlepool
1930			
3 Jan	Joe Lowther	l pts 15	Hull
13 Jan	Joe Lowther	l pts 15	Hull
25 Jan	Jerry Daley	w ret 6	Sunderland
9 Feb	Dick Burt	w pts 12	Leeds
16 Feb	Hal O'Neill	w pts 12	Leeds
22 Feb	Sonny Bird	w pts 15	Sunderland
16 Mar	Hal O'Neill	w ret 8	Leeds
24 Mar	Wattie Wilde	w rsc 5	Hartlepool
29 Mar	Archie Sexton	l pts 15	Sunderland
4 Apr	George Porter	w pts 12	Bradford

11 Apr	Jack Haynes	drew 15	Barnsley
19 Apr	Farmer Jackson	w ret 11	Sunderland
28 Apr	Sandy McKenzie	l pts 15	Hartlepool
3 May	Jack Haynes	w dis 6	Sunderland
12 May	Sandy McKenzie	l pts 15	Newcastle
31 May	Charlie McDonald	l pts 15	Sunderland
13 Jun	Joe Woodruff	w pts 12	Preston
21 Jun	Bert Mottram	w dis 4	Crook
28 Jun	Pat Casey	w ret 7	Newcastle
11 Jul	Roy Martin	w rsc 3	Preston
20 Jul	Fred Oldfield	w ret 5	Leeds
25 Jul	Hal O'Neill	w ret 7	Preston
17 Aug	Joe Lowther	w pts 12	Leeds
20 Aug	Gunner Ainsley	w ret 3	Hartlepool
30 Aug	Ted Coveney	w ret 5	Newcastle
10 Sep	Joe Woodruff	w pts 12	Harrogate
17 Sep	Joe Woodruff	w pts 15	Morecombe
20 Sep	Billy Roberts	w ret 4	Newcastle
30 Sep	Jerry Daley	w ret 6	Manchester
5 Oct	Fred Shaw	w pts 12	Leeds
10 Oct	Joe Lowther	l ret 11	Preston
9 Nov	Harry Mason	l pts 12	Leeds

17 Nov	Sandy McKenzie	l pts 15	Glasgow
9 Dec	Sandy McKenzie	w rsc 7	Manchester
21 Dec	Joe Lowther	w pts 12	Leeds
1931			
1 Jan	Joe Woodruff	w pts 12	Barnsley
3 Jan	Archie Sexton	w ret 9	Manchester
18 Jan	Fred Shaw	l pts 12	Leeds
27 Jan	Jack Hood	l pts 15	Manchester
16 Feb	Phil Green	l pts 10	Newcastle
23 Feb	Fred Shaw	l pts 12	Leeds
2 Mar	Jack O'Brien	w pts 10	Leeds
9 Mar	George Willis	w ret 10	Newcastle
17 Mar	Jack O'Brien	w ret 7	Manchester
22 Mar	Jack O'Brien	w ko 3	Leeds
10 Apr	Jack Haynes	w ko 2	Preston
4 May	George Gordon	w ko 2	Newcastle
6 Jun	Fred Shaw	w ret 12	Barnsley
12 Jun	Jack Haynes	w ko 1	Middlesbrough
29 Jun	Dick Bartlett	w ko 2	Hartlepool
3 Jul	Sonny Doke	w ret 4	Preston
27 Jul	Fred Shaw	drew 15	Hartlepool
3 Aug	Archie Sexton	drew 15	South Shields

5 Aug	Dixie Cullen	w ret 5	Hartlepool
11 Sep	Glen Moody	w rsc 4	Manchester
20 Sep	Fred Shaw	w pts 12	Leeds
19 Oct	Joe Rostron	w rsc 7	Hartlepool
9 Nov	Marcel Thil	l pts 10	London
16 Nov	Joe Woodruff	w rsc 3	Manchester
23 Nov	Bob McGovern	w rsc 3	Newcastle
7 Dec	Harry Mason	w dis 3	Leeds
16 Dec	Seaman Harvey	l pts 6	London
28 Dec	Billy Adair	w ret 3	Newcastle
1932			
18 Jan	Dick Bartlett	w ko 2	Manchester
8 Feb	Len Harvey	l pts 15	Newcastle
14 Mar	Seaman Harvey	w ert 3	Newcastle
1 Apr	Sandy McKenzie	w ko 2	Middlesbrough
8 Apr	Jack Marshall	w rsc 6	Blackburn
22 Apr	Hal O'Neill	w rsc 2	Middlesbrough
6 May	Red Pullen	w ko 5	Hartlepool
27 May	Les Saunders	w ko 4	Nelson
30 May	Glen Moody	w pts 12	Birmingham
9 Jun	Eddie Strawer	w pts 12	Douglas (IofM)
19 Jun	Billy Thomas	w rsc 3	Royton

18 Jul	Jack McAvoy *Northern Area Middleweight title*	w dis 14	Manchester
1 Aug	George Porter	w ko 2	Sunderland
4 Aug	Glen Moody	w ko 2	Hartlepool
3 Oct	Archie Sexton	w ko 7	Newcastle
16 Oct	George Brown	w pts 10	Leeds
31 Oct	Del Fontaine	w ko 4	Newcastle
14 Nov	Glen Moody	w rsc 3	Newcastle
12 Dec	Len Harvey *British Middleweight title*	l pts 15	Newcastle
1933			
9 Jan	Eddie Maguire	w pts 12	Newcastle
27 Jan	Seaman Harvey	w pts 15	Plymouth
6 Feb	Leo Bandias	w ret 12	Newcastle
27 Feb	Eddie Maguire	w ko 3	Newcastle
9 Mar	Eddie Robinson	w rsc 4	Liverpool
13 Mar	Eddie Maguire	l pts 12	Newcastle
10 Apr	Archie Sexton	l pts 12	Manchester
22 Apr	Joe Woodruff	w ret 6	Carlisle
7 May	Les Ward	w ret 5	Royton
24 May	Carmelo Candel	l ret 5	Paris
6 Jun	Dino Guselli	w ret 2	Inverness

12 Jun	Jack London	w ret 10	Hartlepool
26 Jun	Ernie Simmons	l pts 10	Leicester
25 Aug	Billy Wallace	w ret 3	Darlington
3 Sep	Reg Perkins	l pts 12	Middlesbrough
11 Sep	Ernie Simmons	l pts 12	Hartlepool
7 Oct	Johnny Summers	w ret 12	Sunderland
23 Oct	Paul Schaefer	w pts 12	Manchester
3 Nov	Andy McLaughlin	w pts 12	North Shields
11 Dec	Eddie Maguire	drew 15	Hull
1934			
22 Jan	Johnny Summers	w pts 12	York
3 Feb	Les Ward	w ret 3	Sunderland
19 Feb	Bushman Dempster	w ret 6	Edinburgh
13 Mar	Jack Marshall	w ret 6	Ashton under Lyme
19 Mar	Reggie Meen	w dis 7	Newcastle
2 Apr	Dave Sullivan	w ret 2	Ashton under Lyme
9 Apr	Charlie Belanger	w dis 7	Newcastle
23 Apr	Tommy Farr	w pts 12	Newcastle
21 May	George Slack	w pts 10	Newcastle
25 Jul	Erich Seelig	l pts 12	London
27 Aug	Paul Schaefer	l pts 12	Newcastle

10 Sep	Manuel Abrew	l pts 10	Newcastle
9 Oct	Jack Sharkey	w ret 3	Hanley
15 Oct	Bushman Dempster	w pts 12	Carlisle
29 Oct	Phil Monro	w ko 7	Newcastle
12 Nov	Bushman Dempster	w dis 11	Hartlepool
17 Nov	Ginger Hauxwell	w ko 7	Sunderland
5 Dec	Leonard Steyaert	l pts 12	York
17 Dec	Jimmy Tarante	l pts 12	Newcastle
1935			
21 Jan	Charlie Smith	l ret 7	Newcastle
8 Apr	Helmuth Hartkopp	l pts 12	Newcastle
28 May	Jack London	l pts 12	Sunderland
1937			
6 Dec	Jackie Moran	l pts 10	Newcastle
20 Dec	Reggie Meen	w rsc 2	Newcastle
1938			
17 Jan	Ron Lindley	w pts 5	Bradford
31 Jan	Stan Kirby	l pts 10	Darlington
21 Feb	Jim McKenzie	l pts 10	Newcastle
21 Mar	Zachy Nicholas	l pts 10	Penzance
31 Mar	Packy Paul	l ret 3	Sheffield
1942			
22 Feb	Martin Thornton	l rsc 6	Loughborough

CHAPTER THREE

DOUGLAS PARKER

Northern Area Lightweight Champion 1933-35

'By far the heftiest puncher, pound for pound, ever to appear in North East rings was Douglas Parker.' This was the judgement of boxing pundit, Fred Charlton, writing in the 1960s after following the fight game in the North East for over 40 years. [1] Parker could certainly deliver a knock-out punch with either hand as he demonstrated on numerous occasions and this was allied with a dynamic style of fighting. His career had some memorable peaks and some disappointments, yet, win or lose, he rarely failed to excite the fans and his name on a boxing bill guaranteed a good attendance. In 1931, he fought the world bantamweight champion, Panama Al Brown, in a non-title match; and he won the Northern Area Lightweight title in November 1933, holding it until he retired from the ring, in 1935. Parker, however, was disqualified in the final eliminating contest for the British lightweight championship, in the following year, and therefore never fought for a British title. Douglas Parker was sometimes billed with the phrase 'He's a good un!' and even if he did not reach the apex of the boxing profession, there can be no doubt that he was one of the most colourful and exciting fighters of the inter-war years.

Douglas Parker was born in Aberdeen, the son of William and Jessie Parker. His father was the chief engineer on a Scottish fishing trawler. Douglas had two professional fights in Scotland and then joined the staff of a boxing booth in a travelling fair. He came to Sunderland, in August 1927, on board a coastal vessel, intending to stay a few weeks.[2] North East England in the 1920's was a hotbed of boxing, with over a dozen promotions every week and scores of gyms and boxing schools in the area. Young Parker was in his element and his all-action boxing style soon

DOUGLAS PARKER

endeared him to the local fight fans. He liked Sunderland, married a local girl - Elizabeth Conlon, and made his home in the town.

Yet, his early fight record in the area was patchy. He lost his first fight, losing on points to Young Dusty over ten rounds at Chester-le-Street. He stopped Kid Watson in the second round , at Stanley, and was then stopped by Alf Page, at Chester-le-Street, in the fourth round. A win over Ernie Veitch was followed by a defeat by Kid Watson, in a return match at Sunderland. He returned to Scotland for a fight with Frank Parkes, at Dundee, suffering the first knock-out of his career, and on his return to the North East he continued to fight in local arenas. Len Johnson, the boxer and promoter, was then putting on shows at Consett and, in April 1928, he matched Parker with Young Dusty for a third meeting. This time Parker reversed the previous decisions by stopping Dusty in the sixth round. 'Parker is going to be a sensation' forecast Len Johnson after the fight.

On 17 November 1928, Parker faced Jean Locatelli, an Italian with an all-action style to match Parker's, and the Scot knocked him out in the second round. Three fights later, Parker was matched with Hans Lincke from Heidelberg, one of the German boxers then resident on Wearside. Both men survived counts and Parker won the decision on points. In the inevitable return match, a month later, Parker knocked out the German with an uppercut, in the third round. Sid Raiteri from London was then disposed of by Parker in four rounds.

Douglas Parker knew who he wanted next: 'wonder boy' Nipper Pat Daly from Marylebone. The baby-faced Daly was a boxing prodigy. He had been fighting professionally since the age of twelve and had fought 66 bouts, with only six losses, when he was matched with Parker. He was trained and managed by Andy Newton, the son of the celebrated Professor Newton, the author of several books on boxing techniques. The Nipper had already appeared five times, at the Sunderland Stadium, and local favourite, Billy Smith, had been among his victims. Fred Charlton, who was then matchmaker at the Holmeside Stadium, was keen to set up the fight. It was fixed for 8 June 1929 and to be 15 rounds at 8st 9lbs. Parker was paid eight guineas for the bout, his biggest purse to date.

Parker always regarded the Daly fight as one of the peaks of his career. When the opening bell rang, Parker rushed towards Daly's corner and caught him with a left hook to the jaw. Daly struggled up at the count of nine and pushed out his long left to fend off Parker, but the Scot backed him into a corner and caught him with a right to the chin. The Nipper took a count of eight and, when he rose, Parker finished him off with an uppercut. The fight was over in 90 seconds. Daly was carried back to his corner as the crowd went wild. Hats were thrown in the air and many spectators stood on their seats to cheer Parker.

Five fights later, Parker met Benny Sharkey of Newcastle, in the first of their four ring meetings.[3] It was a 15 round contest at 8st 9lbs between two of the North East's up-and-coming fighters. Although Parker did not have it all his own way, he was on top form for most of the contest. Sharkey took counts in the third and eleventh rounds, and in the thirteenth, when Sharkey took another count, there were shouts from some ringsiders that the fight should be stopped to save him from further punishment. There was no towel thrown in from Benny's corner, however, and referee Jimmy Britt allowed the fight to go the full distance with Duggie Parker a clear winner on points.

On 28 September 1929, Douglas Parker faced another local favourite in Billy Smith. Smith was a superb boxer with an outstanding record that showed he lost only six out of 67 contests. He was never knocked down, stopped or disqualified in his entire career. Only premature retirement with stomach trouble prevented him from fighting for a title. The Parker-Smith match was a meeting of fighter versus boxer over 15 rounds, with Billy Smith emerging as the winner. There were many local fans who believed that Parker would be the first man to put Billy Smith down for the full count. Smith, however, had made a very careful study of Parker's style and he successfully slipped Parker's punches and got in counter blows which built up a points lead for him.

On 1 December 1929, Douglas Parker travelled to London for his first fight in the capital, where he outpointed Len Pinkus of Mile End, over 15 rounds at Premierland. A London reporter wrote:

> *'It was a wonderful bout, and many old stagers at the East End Arena said that they had never seen such a fine and exciting fight. Parker displayed a rare knowledge of the game. He has a punch in both hands, and is indeed very clever. His display must be equal to championship form. The Mile End boy is on his own where pluck is concerned. We have seen him in some hectic affairs, but this bout with Parker was about the hottest contest we remember. It looked 10 to 1 on Len upsetting the odds in the 12th round, for he sent Parker flying round the ring. But this Parker is a good general who picked his punches with enjoyable accuracy. Duggie should make a name for himself in London boxing.'*[4]

Over the next 12 months, Douglas Parker had 15 fights, in London, being matched against foreign fighters Francois Machtens, Jules Bodson, Henri Whadlaac and Joe Martinez, and Londoners Al Foreman, Harry Berry and Billy Boulger.

Parker's bout with Al Foreman, at Premierland, brought him up against Foreman's famous - or infamous - boxing gloves. Foreman was born in Aldgate and began his boxing career in London rings under the name Bert Harris. At the age of 17, he joined his brothers in Montreal, fought in North American rings, and won the Canadian lightweight title. In 1929, he returned to Britain as Al Foreman, bringing with him his famous gloves. Foreman had very small hands and it suited him to have his gloves specially made. So, before leaving America, he entered into a contract with the Everlast boxing equipment company, in which he undertook to use their gloves in British rings in return for a free supply of the specially-made gloves, while his opponents would wear the standard Everlast gloves provided free by the company. British promoters were only too happy to receive a free supply of gloves and they did not object to the arrangement. When Parker saw the special gloves, he protested against their use. The offending gloves were weighed and were the right weight - six ounces - but they were obviously smaller than the standard boxing gloves. Furthermore, Foreman declined to be weighed for the fight and his contract showed that he was within his rights to refuse. Douglas Parker was eventually persuaded to enter the ring against an unweighed (and obviously much heavier) opponent wearing a specially-made pair of gloves. Parker's tactics were to go for a quick knock-out and he staggered Foreman with a good left hook early in the fight, but, in the second round, in his eagerness to finish things off, he left himself open to a counter punch and Foreman dropped him for the full count. After these events, managers began to check the small print in contracts before their boxers signed to meet Al Foreman. The Board of Control also began to insist on the use of standard boxing gloves for all boxers and Foreman had to conform to the Board's regulations. It did him no harm for he held the British lightweight title 1930-32. Foreman, apparently, was an affable man outside of boxing but he would use any trick to gain an advantage inside it. Perhaps this was a hangover from the years he spent in American rings.

On 31 May 1930, Douglas Parker shared top billing, at the last night of boxing to be held at the Holmeside Stadium, when he met Billy Smith in a rematch, and Jack Casey took on Charlie

THE STADIUM

SATURDAY, MAY 31st.

DOUGLAS PARKER

v.

BILLY SMITH

CHARLIE McDONALD

v.

JACK CASEY

OTHER CONTESTS.

PRICES:—1/3, 2/4, and 4/9.

Billy Smith and Douglas Parker (in white trunks) sparring for an opening in the eight round of their 15 round contest at the Holmeside Stadium, Sunderland, on 31 May 1930

McDonald. The Stadium had been the scene of many Parker victories - however, he failed to master Billy Smith, who scored a second points victory over the pugnacious Scot.

In January 1931, Parker had the first of three fights against Seaman Tommy Watson. The fight was staged at Kilburn and Parker was outpointed over 15 rounds by the redoubtable tar. Five fights later - a sequence of wins for Parker - the Wearside-based Scot was matched against Al Brown of Panama over 15 rounds at New St James Hall.[5] Brown was the world bantamweight champion. Peter Wilson described him as 'lithe as a great black jaguar' and he rated him the greatest bantamweight he had seen in the ring.[6] Brown had won the title in 1929 and held it until 1935. He was 5ft 11 ins in height with a correspondingly long reach and he could deliver a knock-out punch with either hand. He was a formidable opponent and was strongly favoured to win, but Parker had caused some sensational upsets in the past and his supporters were there in force to cheer him on.

The fight started quietly and Parker did most of the attacking during the first three rounds. Then Brown's long left began to find its target and, in round eight, he brought his right into play and dropped Parker five times. Duggie kept on battling and took another count, in round ten. In the eleventh round, Brown caught him with a perfect right hook which put Parker down for the full count. Douglas Parker had lost but he was certainly not disgraced. Panama Al's manager, Dave Lumiansky, said after the fight: '*I never saw a fighter with so much guts. We had planned a fourth round win and never bargained for the 11 rounds the fight lasted.*'

Parker moved out of the bantamweight class, after this fight, and was soon in action against featherweight opposition. On 14 September 1931, he was matched with Johnny Cuthbert, the British featherweight champion, in a 15 rounds non-title fight, at

New St James Hall. Again, it was a full house at 'St Jim's' as the crowds rolled up to watch Parker pit himself against another title-holder. Parker dominated the fight and dropped the champion for counts of six, in the second and fifth rounds, and, in the tenth round, only the bell saved Cuthbert from being counted out. The end came in the eleventh round, when Parker cracked a right to Cuthbert's jaw. The champion rose at eight but a right to the body put him down for the full count.

After his victory over the champion, Parker could have cashed in on his reputation and picked up a number of relatively easy but lucrative fights across the country, while waiting for a title fight. This would have put cash in his pocket and boosted his fight record. Instead, he insisted on meeting one of the leading contenders for the British featherweight title, his former opponent - Seaman Tommy Watson. Parker was determined to reverse his previous defeat and prove he was the better man. Watson accepted with alacrity, seeing that a victory over Parker would put him in line for a shot at the title. The contest took place at New St James Hall, on 5 October 1931, four days after Nel Tarleton had taken the British featherweight title from Johnny Cuthbert. The Parker-Watson bout, therefore, was an unofficial eliminating contest to see who would challenge Tarleton for the title, and both men knew what was at stake.

Watson relied chiefly on his left jab and he built up a comfortable points lead over the first four rounds, but Parker clipped him on the chin, in the fifth round, and the Geordie seaman took a count of five, and he took another short count in the ninth round. Duggie made his big effort in the eleventh round when he dropped Watson for two counts but failed to finish him off. Both men were weary, after eleven gruelling rounds and, in the twelfth, it was Tommy Watson's turn to catch Parker with a right to the jaw which put him down for a count of nine. On rising, Parker was assailed by a barrage of blows from the sailor and, as

Parker dropped to the canvas, the towel came sailing in from his corner. Seaman Watson went on to take the British title from Nel Tarleton, in the following year, while Parker was stopped inside the distance in both of his non-title contests with Tarleton, in 1932.

Indeed, 1932 was a patchy year for Douglas Parker, caused by weight problems as he outgrew the featherweight division. On 25 January, he met Benny Sharkey for a second meeting, at New St James Hall. This time, it was Sharkey who dictated the fight and he gained a points victory over the Scot. Parker was knocked out by Tarleton, in the seventh round, when they met at Manchester, on 8 February 1932. Three weeks later, Parker faced Benny Sharkey for a third time. In this fight, Parker held a narrow points lead until the thirteenth round when Sharkey landed a good left hand punch on Parker's jaw which sent him crashing to the boards. He made the mistake of rising too soon and Sharkey put him down for a second count. In the fourteenth round, Sharkey was completely on top and, with Parker clutching the ropes for support, the referee stopped the fight and raised Benny's hand. Five weeks later, Parker was outpointed by Tommy Hyams over 10 rounds at the Crystal Palace, but he picked up a couple of wins, over Bert Taylor and Kid Nicholson, and then travelled to Barcelona where he was knocked out by Jose Giranes, in the third round. It was a case of mixed fortunes until November when he put together a sequence of four wins up to the end of the year.

In 1933, Parker consolidated his position in the lightweight class and, with weight problems behind him, he recovered his old form. He also had a new manager in Nick Cavalli. Cavalli was a trainer at the Italian Sporting Club in London's Soho district, and from his office in Greek Street he managed several fighters and acted as an agent for many more. He had wide international contacts and was a prominent figure in the boxing scene of the 1930's. Like many other Italian nationals living in Britain, he was interned as an enemy alien when Italy entered the war, in 1940. Although he had a London-based manager, Douglas Parker remained resident in Sunderland - indeed, he shared a tenement house in Church Walk with Jack Casey - and trained at the Empire gym, in Littlegate, Bishopwearmouth. Cavalli opened negotiations to take Parker to the U.S.A. 'where his whirlwind style will please the Americans', but failed to secure a contract guaranteeing four fights for Parker in American rings and the trip never took place. Cavalli, however, was able to secure some good matches for Parker and the Scot was never idle for long.

On 13 January 1933, Parker was matched with Dom Valente, at Blackfriars Ring, in what Victor Berliner described as the most exciting fight he ever promoted. Berliner had just taken over at the Ring and he recorded that everyone thought him mad to match two Northern fighters - Parker and Valente - on a Sunday afternoon bill at Blackfriars. However, the arena was packed for the bout which turned out to be one big slam from start to finish. In the fifth round, Parker appeared to be on the verge of defeat, when he launched a left hook which lifted Valente off his feet and put him down for a count of six. Valente was unable to come out for the next round, leaving Parker the victor.

On 30 January 1933, Parker met Benny Sharkey in a final encounter. The match was 15 rounds at 9st 6lbs and, as before, the fight was a complete sell-out, at New St James Hall. Parker dropped Sharkey for a count of eight, in the first round, but Benny fought back strongly, in the second, and the third round was even. Sharkey came charging out of his corner throwing punches, in the fourth round, but Parker sidestepped the assault and rammed home a left to the body, which dropped the Novocastrian for the full count - the first time Benny Sharkey had been knocked out in 61 fights.

Nick Cavalli
Douglas Parker's Manager

PUT THESE GREAT FIGHTERS ON YOUR PROGRAMMES.

DOUGLAS PARKER
Will take on any British Light-weight.

JIMMY KNOWLES Challenges any British Bantam.

GUSTAVE ROTH
The uncrowned Middle-weight Champion (I.B.U.) of the World . . . . Recently defeated KID TUNERO, who beat MARCEL THIL.

Here are four Heavy-weights :—

The Best the Continent can produce—THEY CAN BE BACKED WITH GOOD SUBSTANTIAL MONEY—REAL MONEY—AGAINST ANY CHAMPION IN ENGLAND.

CHARLEY BELANGER (Canada)
Official Heavy-weight Champion of Canada.

ISIDORO CASTANAGA (Spain)
K.O.'d Retzaf and other leading Americans.

JOHN ANDERSON (Sweden)
I.B.U. Champion.

GUSTAVE LIMOSIN (Belgium)
Official Challenger for title held by Pierre Charles

These Boxers make money for Promoters and can be backed for real money against the best in the land.

NICK CAVALLI,
ITALIAN SPORTING CLUB,
15, GREEK STREET, LONDON, W.1

On 25 February, Parker travelled to Brussels where he was outpointed by Francois Sybille over ten rounds, and, a month later, he drew with the Frenchman, Fernand Viez, at the Albert Hall, but he scored some wins over British opposition, and, on 6 November, met Jim Learoyd for the Northern Area lightweight title, at New St James Hall. Learoyd, from Leeds, had won the title the previous year and this was his first defence. The fight lacked thrills until the fourteenth round when Parker caught the Yorkshireman with a left hook. Learoyd took a count of nine and, when he got up, Parker pursued him round the ring, bombarding him with lefts and rights. Learoyd, however, refused to go down and the referee intervened to save him from taking any more blows. On 27 November, Parker knocked out the Scottish lightweight champion, Tommy Spiers, in the second round, demonstrating that he could have been the Scottish champion if he had not chosen to take up residence in Sunderland and fight for the Northern Area title.

On 5 February 1934, Douglas Parker met Welsh champion, Billy Quinlan, in a final eliminator for the British lightweight title then held by Harry Mizler. The fight was staged at New St James Hall and it was one of the most important in Parker's boxing career. Both men boxed cautiously, for the first two rounds, but in round three, Parker dropped Quinlan for a count of six and, when the Welshman rose, Parker tore into him with both hands. Quinlan, however, was not overwhelmed by Parker's wild assault and he did some effective counter punching. In round four, Parker put Quinlan down for a count of nine, but Quinlan was far from finished and he caught Parker with a right swing which almost knocked him out of the ring. In the words of one reporter "they fought like a couple of demons". In round five, they continued to slog it out and brought the crowd to its feet with excitement. Early in round six, Parker landed a body punch on Quinlan which the referee judged to be a foul blow, and he disqualified Parker. There was uproar at this decision, many spectators claiming that the punch had been above the belt. The referee thought otherwise, however, and his judgement was the one that mattered. Some observers believed that if Parker had kept a cool head he could have finished Quinlan off in either round three or four and thereby earned the right to meet Harry Mizler in a British lightweight title fight.

Instead of touching a new peak, Douglas Parker's career went into a decline. Over the next 18 months, he had 20 fights and lost 16 of them. One of his four wins was a lacklustre defence of his Northern Area lightweight title against Newcastle's Norman Dale, on 25 November 1934. After 11 dull rounds, Dale had Parker in trouble in the twelfth round but failed to move in on him, and Duggie came back strongly over the last three rounds to gain a points decision. Parker's name on a boxing bill continued to draw crowds but he was now past his best and he retired from the ring, in July 1935.

Shortly after his retirement, Douglas Parker took ill with blood poisoning. He had to undergo an operation and had long spells in hospital. With their breadwinner unemployed and the need to meet hospital bills, these were not easy times for the Parker family and, on 12 December 1935, George Jackson, the promoter at Sunderland's Royal Stadium, organised a benefit evening for the ex-boxer. Jack Casey and Arthur Clarey, Billy and Tom Smith, and Seaman Tommy Watson and Billy Charlton boxed exhibition bouts and there was an open featherweight competition with the prize of a silver cup for the winner. J.J.Paget, the Newcastle promoter, also arranged a ringside collection for Parker, at New St James Hall. A treasured oil portrait of Parker in fighting pose, painted when he was in his prime, was auctioned by Duggie to raise money for his family.

Douglas Parker was sufficiently recovered to join the Army, in 1939, and he became a sergeant in the Pioneer Corps. He took part in some Army boxing tournaments and acted as a boxing instructor but he, wisely, never attempted a come-back in the professional ring. On his discharge, he worked as a plater's helper in Shorts shipyard and, in 1950, he took a job working on the screens, at Wearmouth colliery, until bad health forced his retirement, in 1961. Douglas Parker never courted the limelight and was rarely seen at boxing shows after his retirement. He was a man of few words and rarely talked about his ring exploits, although he gave boxing instruction at a local boys' club for many years. His last years were marred by poor health and he collapsed at his home, in Friar Road, Ford Estate, on 29 November 1965, and he died the next day, at Ryhope General Hospital. He was survived by his wife Elizabeth and his two sons and two daughters.

General Manager
Victor Berliner.

Doors Open 2 p.m.

THE RING

BLACKFRIARS ROAD, S.E.1.

Advance Booking—
Hop 5966-7.

Commence 3 p.m.

SUNDAY, JANUARY 1st, 1933.

SMASHING ATTRACTIONS FOR NEW YEAR'S DAY.

Four Fifteen Round Contests

WILLIE UNWIN (SOUTH AFRICA) v. **DEL FONTAINE** (CANADA)

EVAN LANE (WALES) v. **DOUGLAS PARKER** (SUNDERLAND)

TOMMY HYAMS (KING'S CROSS) v. **TOM THOMAS** (WALES)

JOHNNY PETERS (BATTERSEA) v. **BERT TAYLOR** (BIRMINGHAM)

Book Now. 1/10, 3/6 Unr. Ringside or Balcony, 6/-, 8/6, 12/- Res.

General Manager
Victor Berliner.

Doors Open 2 p.m.

THE RING

BLACKFRIARS ROAD, S.E.1.

Advance Booking—
Hop 5966-7.

Commence 3 p.m.

SUNDAY, JANUARY 15th, 1933.

ANOTHER COLOSSAL PROGRAMME THAT SMASHES ALL PREVIOUS RECORDS.
WE DEFY YOU TO NAME ONE WINNER WITH CONFIDENCE.

Imperial Cruiser-weight Clash 15 ROUNDS

WILLIE UNWIN (SOUTH AFRICA) v. **DEL FONTAINE** (CANADA)

Smashing 15 ROUNDS Light-weight Thriller

DOM VOLANTE (LIVERPOOL) v. **DOUGLAS PARKER** (SUNDERLAND)

Extra Special 15 ROUNDS Cruiser-weight Bout

TED MASON (MAIDSTONE) v. **JACK O'MALLEY** (AUSTRALIA)

Extra Special 15 ROUNDS Feather-weight Bout

PHINEAS JOHN (WALES) v. **JIM GORDON** (DARLINGTON)

Book Now. 1/10, 3/6 Unr. Ringside or Balcony, 6/-, 8/6, 12/- Res.

LIVERPOOL STADIUM (Adjoining EXCHANGE STATION)

THE FINEST BOXING HALL IN GREAT BRITAIN

TO-MORROW, THURSDAY, MARCH 16th, at 7.45 LIVERPOOL STADIUM LTD. PRESENT
(Under the Direction of Johnny Best)

FIFTEEN Three-Minute Rounds Contest at 9st. 9lb. Weigh in at 2 p.m.

DOUGLAS PARKER SUNDERLAND v. **JIMMY STEWART** LIVERPOOL

TWELVE Three-Minute Rounds Contest at 10st.

GEO. (PANTHER) PURCHASE Light-weight Champion of South Africa v. **HAROLD HIGGINSON** Liverpool's Popular Light-weight

TEN Three-Minute Rounds Contest

TOMMY WALSH Liverpool v. **JIMMY CLOUGH** Earlstown

TEN Three-Minute Rounds Contest

YOUNG SANDERSON Liverpool v. **BILLY McCAMLEY** Scotland

Also Other Contests. Tickets Obtained at:—STADIUM (Telephone: Bank 4727); Ladies Admitted.
JACK SHARP, Whitechapel; RUSHWORTH & DREAPER, Islington; PIED BULL HOTEL, Chester.

RESERVED. All Bookable Seats.

Prices of Admission (including Tax.)	Ringside	Extension	Circle	Outer Circle	Unreserved
	7/6	5/-	3/6	2/6	1/6

DOUGLAS PARKER'S RING RECORD 1927-35

1927			
23 Mar	Jim Ingram	w ko 2	Aberdeen
13 Apr	Young Tweedie	w rsc 7	Dundee
26 Aug	Young Dusty	l pts 10	Chester-le-Street
2 Sep	Kid Watson	w rsc 2	West Stanley
9 Sep	Alf Page	l ret 4	Chester-le-Street
17 Sep	Ernie Veitch	w pts 15	Tyne Dock
24 Sep	Kid Watson	l ret 5	Sunderland
28 Sep	Frank Parkes	l ko 5	Dundee
8 Oct	Young Thomas	w rsc 4	Newcastle
22 Oct	Buck Dryden	l ret 5	West Stanley
5 Nov	Billy Farrell	l ret 2	Newcastle
19 Nov	Jack Clayton	w pts 15	Washington
21 Nov	Jack Clayton	l rsc 6	Newcastle
3 Dec	Young Dusty	l rsc 7	Sunderland
30 Dec	Freddie Hughes	w pts 10	Aberdeen
1928			
17 Mar	Alf Page	l pts 10	Sunderland
21 Mar	Jim Dottle	l ko 4	Tyne Dock
26 Mar	Bob Southern	l pts 15	Darlington
7 apr	Alf Page	w ret 8	Sunderland

9 Apr	Young Dusty	w rsc 6	Consett
16 Apr	George Harwood	drew 10	Consett
14 May	Jack Clayton	w pts 15	Darlington
21 May	Young Graham	l ko 9	Consett
26 May	Andy Keating	l pts 10	Hetton-le-Hole
2 Jun	George Harwood	l ko 9	Darlington
26 Sep	George Ballantyne	w ko 8	Dundee
22 Oct	Ted Cullen	l dis 4	Darlington
2 Nov	Young Josephs	w pts 10	Darlington
9 Nov	Young Graham	l pts 12	Ashington
17 Nov	Jean Locatelli	w ko 2	Sunderland
17 Dec	Peter Cuthbertson	l pts 10	Edinburgh
1929			
11 Jan	Kid Abrahams	w pts 15	Darlington
14 Jan	Benny McGhee	l pts 10	Edinburgh
19 Jan	Hans Lincke	w pts 12	Sunderland
28 Jan	Young Graham	l pts 12	Ashington
16 Feb	Hans Lincke	w ko 3	Sunderland
23 Feb	Johnny Summers	drew 15	Sunderland
11 Mar	Sonny Chappell	w rsc 11	South Shields
19 Mar	Freddie Hughes	l pts 12	Edinburgh
23 Mar	Danny Finn	w rsc 8	Newcastle

13 Apr	Young Josephs	w pts 15	Newcastle
15 Apr	Jack Kelly	w pts 15	South Shields
4 May	Jack Bates	w pts 15	Newcastle
11 May	Sid Raiteri	w rsc 4	Sunderland
12 May	Tommy Rice	w ko 1	Leeds
26 May	Jack Ellis	w ret 3	Leeds
28 May	Jack Glover	l pts 15	Newcastle
8 Jun	Nipper Pat Daly	w ko 1	Sunderland
20 Jun	Jack Moody	w rsc 10	Liverpool
23 Jun	Kid Nicholson	l pts 15	Leeds
28 Jun	Bert Taylor	l pts 12	Preston
6 Jul	Len Fowler	w pts 15	Sunderland
3 Aug	Kid Socks	w pts 15	Sunderland
17 Aug	Benny Sharkey	w pts 15	Sunderland
7 Sep	Frank Markey	l pts 15	Sunderland
25 Sep	Kid Socks	w pts 15	Dundee
28 Sep	Billy Smith	l pts 15	Sunderland
21 Oct	Joe Greenwood	drew 15	South Shields
9 Nov	Joe Greenwood	w ret 6	Sunderland
23 Nov	Jack Riley	w pts 15	Sunderland
1 Dec	Lew Pinkus	w pts 15	London
15 Dec	Francois Machtens	l pts 15	London

29 Dec	Francois Machtens	w pts 15	London
1930			
12 Jan	Jules Bodson	w ko 7	London
26 Jan	Lew Pinkus	w pts 15	London
1 Feb	Jack Harris	w ret 9	Sunderland
9 Feb	Henri Whadlaac	w ret 4	London
24 Feb	Lew Pinkus	w pts 15	Leeds
1 Mar	Jack Harris	w pts 15	Sunderland
9 Mar	Joseph Martinez	w rsc 1	London
15 Mar	Billy Reynolds	w ko 3	Sunderland
23 Mar	Al Foreman	l ko 2	London
26 Mar	Gunboat Smith	w ko 1	Aberdeen
12 Apr	Frank Markey	w pts 15	Sunderland
26 Apr	Arthur Lloyd	w ko 2	Sunderland
7 May	Peter Cuthbertson	l pts 15	Aberdeen
12 May	Tommy Lye	w ret 9	Hartlepool
14 May	Frank Markey	w pts 15	Aberdeen
31 May	Billy Smith	l pts 15	Sunderland
23 Jun	Tommy Rose	w ko 2	Newcastle
30 Jun	Billy Farrell	l pts 15	Newcastle
22 Jul	Dave Parry	w ret 7	Portobello
21 Aug	Kid Pattenden	w rsc 15	London

31 Aug	Harry Berry	w ret 2	London
11 Sep	Charlie Rowbottom	l ret 10	London
2 Oct	Billy Boulger	w pts 15	London
6 Oct	Len Wickwar	w ko 2	Tyne Dock
12 Oct	Evan Lane	drew 15	London
19 Oct	Evan Lane	l pts 15	Londeon
5 Nov	Charlie Rowbottom	drew 15	London
14 Nov	Teddy Brown	l ko 6	Newcastle
1931			
18 Jan	Seaman Tommy Watson	l pts 15	London
26 Jan	Harold Ratchford	w pts 15	Newcastle
1 Feb	Bert Taylor	w pts 15	London
20 Feb	Teddy Brown	w pts 15	Newcastle
7 Mar	Jim Boyle	w pts 15	Newcastle
16 Mar	Kid Nicholson	w rsc 5	Manchester
23 Mar	Panama Al Brown	l ko 11	Newcastle
30 Mar	Seaman Tommy Watson	l pts 15	Newcastle
20 Apr	Cuthbert Taylor	w pts 15	Manchester
11 May	Harold Ratchford	w pts 15	Ashington
18 May	Billy Evans	w ko 7	Manchester
23 May	Harold Ratchford	w pts 15	Ashington

1 Jun	Nel Tarleton	l pts 8	London
10 Jun	Nick Bensa	w pts 12	Oxford
5 Aug	Sonny Lee	w ko 4	Hartlepool
23 Aug	Francois Machtens	l pts 12	Leeds
31 Aug	Phineas John	w ko 11	Newcastle
14 Sep	Johnny Cuthbert	w ko 11	Newcastle
5 Oct	Seaman Tommy Watson	l ret 12	Newcastle
2 Nov	Francois Machtens	w pts 15	Newcastle
30 Nov	Dom Volante	l ret 5	Newcastle
1932			
25 Jan	Benny Sharkey	l pts 15	Newcastle
8 Feb	Nel Tarleton	l ko 7	Manchester
29 Feb	Benny Sharkey	l rsc 14	Newcastle
4 Apr	Tommy Hyams	l pts 10	London
25 Apr	Bert Taylor	w pts 12	Newcastle
1 May	Kid Nicholson	w rsc 3	Leeds
11 May	Jose Girones	l ko 1	Barcelona
22 Jun	Jim Cameron	l dis 3	Aberdeen
29 Jun	Jim Cameron	w ko 1	Aberdeen
13 Jul	Jim Cowie	w pts 15	Aberdeen
21 Aug	Jim Learoyd	l pts 12	Middlesbrough
3 Oct	Billy Sheldon	w ret 6	Newcastle
16 Oct	Nel Tarleton	l rsc 10	London

2 Nov	Peter Cuthbertson	w ret 7	Aberdeen
6 Nov	Kid Farlo	w ko 2	London
9 Nov	Jim Bird	w ret 6	Newcastle
12 Dec	Selwyn Davies	w ko 10	London
1933			
1 Jan	Evan Lane	l ko 9	London
15 Jan	Dom Valante	w rsc 6	London
19 Jan	Kid Farlo	w ko 6	London
30 Jan	Benny Sharkey	w ko 4	Newcastle
6 Feb	Dom Valante	w ret 6	Manchester
13 Feb	Jim Travis	w ko 4	Newcastle
25 Feb	Francois Sybille	l pts 10	Brussels
8 Mar	Ginger Jones	drew 8	Cheltenham
16 Mar	Jimmy Stewart	l ret 8	Liverpool
30 Mar	Fernand Viez	drew 10	London
22 May	Sol Soverns	w ko 1	Newcastle
11 Sep	Charlie Barlow	w ret 5	Manchester
6 Nov	Jim Learoyd *Northern Area Lightweight title*	w rsc 14	Newcastle
27 Nov	Tommy Spiers	w ko 2	Newcastle
9 Dec	Jim Bird	w pts 12	Sunderland
14 Dec	Boyo Rees	l rsc 6	Liverpool

1934 5 Feb	Billy Quinlan	l dis 6	Newcastle
26 Feb	Jim Bird	w dis 8	Newcastle
8 Apr	Harry Brooks	l rsc 3	London
30 Apr	Harry Brooks	l pts 10	Newcastle
6 May	Robert Disch	l rsc 12	London
3 Jun	Harry Brook	l pts 10	London
23 Jul	Fred Carpenter	w ko 2	Newcastle
20 Aug	Fred Carpenter	l dis 1	Newcastle
8 Sep	Albert Holding	l dis 2	Sunderland
24 Sep	Norman Dale *Northern Area Lightweight title*	w pts 15	Newcastle
28 Oct	Fred Carpenter	l pts 10	London
3 Dec	Frank Brown	l pts 12	Manchester
17 Dec	Billy Quinlan	l pts 12	Newcastle
1935 27 Jan	Harry Craster	l ret 5	Middlesborough
18 Feb	Alberto Paderni	l rsc 6	Newcastle
4 Mar	Camille Desmet	l pts 12	London
21 Mar	Jock Davie	l ret 2	Glasgow
1 Apr	Johnny Mack	l ret 4	Newcastle
21 Apr	Fred Carpenter	w rsc 9	London
8 Jun	Harry Craster	l pts 10	Sunderland
21 Jul	Tommy Steele	l ret 8	Newcastle

CHAPTER FOUR

ROY MILLS

Northern Area Middleweight Champion 1936-37

After he had retired from the ring, Roy Mills liked nothing better than to talk about his boxing career, which spanned the years 1929-47. During his years in the ring, he boxed at every weight from flyweight to heavyweight, and he fought at many venues, ranging from the humble Byker Bridge 'shack' to top arenas, such as the Empire Hall, Earls Court, and the Ulster Hall, Belfast. He was a good ring craftsman, skilled in defence and attack, with a polished straight left and a lethal left hook. He had confidence in his own abilities and was no respecter of reputations. Boxing pundit, Fred Charlton, considered that Roy Mills was at his best when he fought as a welterweight. It was at this weight that he beat the reigning Scottish, Welsh and Irish champions, and defeated the British welterweight champion in a non-title fight. However, he fought as a middleweight for five years of his career and it was as a middleweight that he fought his way through a series of eliminating bouts to win the Northern Area title, in 1936.

Born in Monkwearmouth, on 12 July 1913, the son of Watson Raymond and Mary Lane Mills, he was christened Emmanuel. His father died when he was very young and therefore had little influence on his son's life. His grandfather and one of his uncles are known to have been bare-knuckle fighters and, if the theories of heredity have any truth in them, perhaps he inherited his aptitude for boxing from them.

The young Mills's early sporting activities, however, were diving, swimming and football. He won no fewer than 17 medals and seven certificates for diving, and successfully competed in many

ROY MILLS

swimming galas. He was also good at football, playing for North Sands in the Wearside League and winning several medals with the club. Then he gravitated to boxing, learning the rudiments at St Cuthbert's Institute in Monkwearmouth, and adding the professional touches at Jack Casey's Moss Lane gym, in the East End of the town.

He had his first professional fight at the Bridge End gym, known as the 'shack', in Byker, on 11 January 1929, at the age of sixteen, when he lost on points to Mickey McGuire over six rounds. He was billed as Boy Mills, in his early fights, but there were so many young boxers at that time calling themselves 'Boy' that the British Boxing Board placed a ban on its use and insisted that boxers choose a proper name. In Mills's case the 'Boy' was changed by a stroke of the pen to 'Roy' and thereafter he was never known by any other name. It must be said that 'Roy Mills' had a good sound to it, and many would consider that he was fortunate to have been able to shed his real name 'Emmanuel'.

His second opponent in the ring was Boy McLoughlin, who was forced to retire in the second round, and in the following week he lost a rematch with Mickey McGuire. A month later, Mills drew with Jarrow's Banty Nipper over six rounds in one of the preliminary fights to the top of the bill contest between Douglas Parker and Nipper Pat Daly, at the Holmeside Stadium. He then lost on points decisions to Peter Veitch and Bob Francis, and ended the year by travelling to the Tudor Stadium, at Blyth, where he gained a points victory over Kid Summers.

Over the years 1930-33, Roy Mills moved up into the ten and twelve rounders and, as his body matured, he moved up the divisions into the lightweight class. Looking back on his career, after retirement, Roy Mills rated his ten rounds points victory over Hamilton's Frank Markey, in 1933, as one of the best performances of his years in the ring. Markey was billed as the

Scottish bantamweight champion. Mills was only nineteen years of age and in his fourth year of professional boxing, when he turned in a brilliant display to take the decision.

Roy Mills used to tell two amusing anecdotes of when he fought in Hartlepool rings during this period. In the summer of 1931, he tackled Alf Craster (cousin of Harry) in a ten round contest at the 'Pools. The match took place in a marquee and a sudden storm blew down the big tent, and with the torn canvas flapping in the wind and rain the two boxers carried on fighting until the final bell. *"The promoter said we deserved a medal each for finishing the contest in those conditions,"* : said Roy, *"Craster and I were like a couple of dead rats at the finish."*

Two years later, on 12 June 1933, he fought George Bunter in an open-air contest held in the Engineers' Club grounds at West Hartlepool. The pair provided the closing bout to the Jack Casey - Jack London top of the bill, which was fought in torrential rain. The crowd kept their seats until Casey had been awarded the decision over big Jack, but once they had seen the main bout of the day, the drenched spectators left the stadium as quickly as they could. Mills and Bunter fought for ten rounds in a deserted, rain-swept stadium, and the referee declared the result a draw.

This was the first of Roy Mills's four contests with George Bunter. Both were welterweights on their way up and the fact that they came from neighbouring towns added a touch of local rivalry to their meetings. Mills and Bunter were matched for a second time at New St James Hall, on 21 January 1935. Mills was ahead on points when he landed a left hook on Bunter's body. The referee ruled that it had landed below the belt and he disqualified Mills for a foul blow. The referee's decision was controversial with the crowd, and the two men were brought together a week later to fight again. After ten rounds, which most spectators thought Mills had won, the same referee, Hymie Gordon,

Roy Mills shakes hands with George Bunter at the weigh-in prior to their fight at the Festival Hall, West Hartlepool, on 18 March 1935.

declared the result a draw. Mills was upset by the decision and, in the heat of the moment, he declared that he felt like retiring from the ring. The two men were matched again, two months later, over 12 rounds at Hartlepool and, after a closely fought bout, George Bunter was awarded the decision. The score was two draws and two wins for Bunter, yet the margins were very close.

George Bunter's real name was Harry Lee. He was a shipyard worker from West Hartlepool who trained alongside Jack London, Jack Strongbow, Dick Bartlett and Al Capone, in the famous school of physical culture run by Tommy Craggs. He made his ring debut at the Redworth Street Stadium, in 1933, and went on to defeat two reigning British welterweight champions - Harry Mason and Pat Butler - in non-title fights, yet he never got a crack at either a British or Northern Area title. George Bunter was undoubtedly one of the North East's leading welterweight fighters of the 1930's. He was certainly Roy Mills's bogey.

In 1934, Mills had 18 fights, winning 14, losing three, with one drawn bout. His wins included points victories over Frank McCall, the Scottish welterweight champion, and Jack McKnight, the Irish welterweight champion. In the following year, he had wins over Pat Butler, the British welterweight champion, Ivor Pickens, the Welsh welterweight champion, and Len Tiger Smith, a former British welterweight title holder. Among his losses was a points defeat at the hands of Ernie Roderick, a future welterweight champion. A boxing reporter saw this defeat as "a severe check to his championship ambitions", but, in 1936, Mills moved up into the middleweights and three good wins soon established him as one of the leading contenders for the Northern Area middleweight title.

In February 1936, the Board of Control ruled that Roy Mills should meet Cock Moffitt of Liverpool in an eliminating bout, the

The former Albion Road Stadium in North Shields where Roy Mills and Tom Smith topped the bill in the 1930s. The building is now used for offices and storerooms.

winner of this contest to meet the winner of a bout between Bob Simpkins and Charlie Parkin, and the winner of the final eliminating contest would be matched with Tommy Moore of Royston, holder of the Northern Area title.

Roy Mills met the local favourite, Cock Moffitt, at Liverpool, on 22 April 1936, in what was described as 'a rousing battle, full of thrills'. Mills abandoned his usual style and slugged it out with the Merseysider, until the eighth round when, after a clash of heads which left Moffitt reeling round the ring with a badly cut eye, the referee stopped the fight. Mills's performance against Bob Simpkins in the final eliminator was one of the best of his career. Mills used his left hook to great effect, and, as Simpkins saw the fight slipping away from him, he went all out in the closing rounds to land a knock-out blow. Mills was able to counter these attacks and, in the final round, he landed with a right cross of his own which put Simpkins on the canvas. Simpkins beat the count, but he lost the fight on points, and Mills won the right to meet Tommy Moore for the Northern title.

The Northern Area championship fight took place four months later, at North Shields, and Mills was in devastating form. He weakened Moore with a series of left hooks to the body, before knocking him out with a right cross to the jaw in the fourth round. *Boxing* magazine awarded Mills its Certificate of Merit for the best performance of the week, and this point must mark the peak of Roy Mills's boxing career. The convincing manner in which he had fought his way through the eliminating bouts and then won the title was the mark of a true champion. Furthermore, he had been the underdog in his fights against Moffitt, Simpkins and Moore, but Roy Mills was never one to be overawed by an opponent and he had the right temperament for the big occasion.

For his next fight, Mills was matched with Tommy Martin, a highly-rated coloured fighter from Deptford, who shortly

Group at the weigh-in of Roy Mills and Bob Simpkins for their final elimination contest for the Northern Area middleweight title at the Royal Stadium, Sunderland. Jack McBeth, matchmaker, is on the extreme left of the group and George Jackson, promoter, stands to the right of Mills.

afterwards moved up into the cruiserweight class. The contest took place at the Empress Hall, Earls Court, and Mills accepted the fight as a late stand-in for Reg Gregory. Top of the bill was a heavyweight contest between Jack London and Larry Gains. The Mills-Martin match was an eight round preliminary bout for which Mills was paid 90 guineas, the biggest purse of his boxing career up to that time. Martin was a good class fighter with a 7lb weight advantage over Mills, and although Mills was too tough and cagey to suffer a knock-out, he took a lot of punishment from the heavier man and lost on points. In his last fight of the year, Mills lost to Darkie Ellis, retiring in the fourth round with an injured hand.

In March 1937, Roy Mills successfully defended his Northern Area title by outpointing Charlie Parkin over 15 rounds, at Sutton-in Ashfield, but five months later, he lost it to Parkin, at New St James Hall, Newcastle. Mills appeared to be coasting to another points win over Parkin, after a dour battle, when, in the twelfth round, he delivered a left hook to Parkin's body followed by a right to the jaw, which dropped Parkin in a heap on the floor. However, instead of starting to count, the referee ordered Mills to his corner and informed the Wearsider that he had been disqualified for a low blow. The punch was borderline but the referee had warned Mills twice before to keep his punches up and no doubt felt that he had to act decisively the third time it happened. It was an unsatisfactory way to lose his title and he never got the chance of winning it back.

By the beginning of 1938, Roy Mills was a 'super middleweight', weighing in at 12 stone for his fight with Butcher Gascoigne, at Sheffield, in March, and this increase in weight led to the only knock-out defeat in Roy Mills's entire boxing career. He was asked by the Merseyside promoter, Johnny Best, to go back into the ring at only four days notice against Liverpool's Ernie Roderick. Mills was a popular performer on Merseyside and he was regarded as a suitable last-minute opponent for the country's leading welterweight contender who sometimes took on middleweights. The fight was within the middleweight limit and it involved Mills in a drastic weight reduction exercise. Mills spent hours in a Turkish bath in order to make the weight, with the result that he entered the ring as weak as a kitten and was knocked out by Roderick in the second round.

A fortnight later, he was matched with Wally Pack from Hoxton at the Empress Hall, Earls Court, in an eight round preliminary fight to the top of the bill contest between Scotland's Benny Lynch and Aurel Toma of Rumania. Pack was a former ABA welterweight champion who had joined the professional ranks as a middleweight. Mills was chosen to give the youngster a stiff test, which Pack came through by forcing Mills's retirement in the fourth round. Again, Mills was weakened by making the weight and he boxed below his best form. In retrospect, the Roderick and Pack fights were both matches which Mills should have declined on weight grounds, although Roy Mills was not the first boxer to believe that he could win the battle of the scales.

Things picked up for Mills, in 1939, after his run of bad results the previous year. In better physical shape, he started the year with wins over Jackie Moran, Dick Freezer, Miles Connolly, and Jack McKnight, before he lost points decisions to Ginger Sadd and the Canadian fighter, Yorky Bentley, and was forced to retire with a cut eye in the fifth round against Len Harrison. A points win over Jack Hart was followed by a points defeat at the hands of Scottish middleweight champion, Bert Gilroy.

On 3 January 1940, Roy Mills was forced to retire in the sixth round in a rematch with Bert Gilroy, and in the following month he lost a points decision to South Shields southpaw, Jim Berry. He beat Gateshead's Sam Sproston and lost to Len Harrison on a disqualification. Then, on 11 May, he met Charlie Parkin, the

Northern Area middleweight champion, the man who had taken the title from him, in a non-title fight at the Pottery Buildings, Sunderland. Mills weighed in at 11st 6lbs for this fight, and looking fit and sharp he knocked out the champion in the fourth round. On 1 June, he again topped the bill at the Pottery Buildings in the last boxing promotion to be staged at this venue, when he defeated Doncaster's George Wells, the referee stopping the contest in the second round. Mills fitted in a fight against Jim Laverick at New St James Hall before he joined the Royal Navy.

In 1942, Seaman Roy Mills was stationed in Northern Ireland and he managed to fit in three fights in Belfast. On 15 July 1942, he topped the bill at the Ulster Hall in a ten round bout with Pat Mulcahy from Cork, the middleweight champion of Eire. Mills was now a fully-fledged cruiserweight and was a stone heavier than his Irish opponent. The referee stopped the fight in the seventh round after Mills sustained a badly cut eye. On 12 September, Mills faced Slough's Jack 'Tiny' Wright in an eight round heavyweight contest, at the Rialto. Mills gave away three stone to his opponent, who weighed in at 15st.13½lb, but Roy knocked him out in the second round. A fortnight later, at the same venue, Roy Mills and Pat Mulcahy met in a rematch, and after 'a rousing display over eight rounds' the referee declared the result a draw. A few months after this fight, Pat Mulcahy, although a natural middleweight, became heavyweight champion of Eire.

These three fights in Northern Ireland were the only ones Roy Mills had in the professional ring during his war service, although he participated in several Royal Navy boxing tournaments. He was only 27 when he joined the Navy and, in the normal course of events, should have had several years of boxing ahead of him, and it is interesting to speculate how he would have fared among the light heavyweights. The evidence suggests he could have held his own with the best in the country, without making a breakthrough to a British championship fight, although he might have been given a crack at the Northern Area title.

After the war, Roy Mills returned to working in the shipyards, and in April 1947, he was tempted back into the ring in a six round heavyweight bout against Bob McArdle, at New St James Hall. McArdle, a tough heavyweight from Barnsley, was no pushover but Mills showed that he had lost none of his ring skills and he boxed his way to a points win over the Yorkshireman. This was the last fight of Roy Mills's boxing career. His interest in boxing never waned; he was a regular attender at boxing matches staged in the area and became an active member of the Sunderland Ex-Boxers Association. He died of a sudden heart attack at his home in Hexham Road, Hylton Lane, on 4 January 1981, and a memorial service was held at St Peter's Church, on the old 'Barbary Coast' where he was born.

Roy Mills at an Ex-Boxers' Association social evening.

BOXING Phone 2552

ROYAL STADIUM, SUNDERLAND
SATURDAY—7.30
Great Twelve Rounds
ROY MILLS v. JOHNNY MELIA
(Sunderland) (Bradford)
Ten Rounds
Billy Lawrence v. Jack Hart
(Ryhope) ((Jarrow)
OTHER CONTESTS
Prices: 6d, 1/- 1/6.

LIVERPOOL STADIUM (Adjoining EXCHANGE STATION)
FINEST BOXING HALL IN GREAT BRITAIN

LIVERPOOL STADIUM LTD. PRESENTS (under the Direction of JOHNNY BEST) **To-morrow, Thursday, Apr. 16th. at 7.45 p.m.**

Official Eliminating Contest for the Northern Area Middle-weight Title
15 3-min. ROUNDS at 11 st. 6 lb. Weigh-in 2 p.m.

COCK MOFFITT (Liverpool) **v. ROY MILLS** (Sunderland)

The hard hitting local middle-weight. Beaten Eddie Maguire (South African Champion)

The clever, Northern Middle-weight who has fought Ernie Roderick, Dave McLeave, Ivor Pickens, and many others

8 3-min. ROUNDS HEAVY-WEIGHT CONTEST

JACK STANNER (WIDNES) v. **HARRY BRIARS** (ST. HELENS)

Winner of the [illegible] Wembley Novice Competition — Beaten Al Conquest and Arthur Holsgrove

AND OTHER CONTESTS

TICKETS obtainable at the STADIUM, 'Phone: Bank 4818 (2 lines), and Agencies. LADIES ADMITTED
The Management reserve the right to refuse admission.

PRICES OF ADMISSION (Including Tax) Ring-side 7/6 — Extension 5/- Circle 3/6 Reserved and Bookable — Outer Circle 2/6 — Unreserved 1/3 Pay at Door

---

BOXING
POTTERY BUILDINGS,
SATURDAY AT 7.15.

CHARLIE PARKIN v. ROY MILLS
(Northern Champion) (Sunderland)
They box ten 3's at 11st. 12lb.

JACK TODD v. BOB BENNETT.
PAT CURRAN v. BILLY BARRAS.
JOE McMULLEN v. OWEN HUGHES.
JIM TRAVERS v. HARRY BELL

Admission 1/- —— 2/-.

ROY MILLS'S RING RECORD 1929-47

1929			
11 Jan	Mickey McGuire	l pts 6	Newcastle
16 Mar	Boy McLaughlin	w rtd 2	Sunderland
25 Mar	Mickey McGuire	l pts 6	Newcastle
8 Jun	Banty's Nipper	drew 6	Sunderland
12 Aug	Young Coulson	w pts 6	Hartlepool
17 Aug	Peter Veitch	l pts 6	Sunderland
24 Aug	Bob Francis	l pts 6	Wheatley Hill
21 Dec	Kid Summers	w pts 6	Blyth
1930			
1 Jan	Tot Murray	drew 10	Hartlepool
3 Feb	Farmer Grimes	w ko 3	Felling
17 Feb	Young Busty	w pts 6	Felling
24 Feb	Ginger Rennie	l pts 10	Hartlepool
8 Mar	Boy McLeod	w pts 6	Sunderland
10 Mar	Young Busty	w pts 10	Tyne Dock
29 Mar	Joe Cowley	w pts 10	Sunderland
7 Jun	Boy Hudson	w pts 6	Newcastle
23 Jun	Mickey McGuire	l pts 6	Newcastle
1 Dec	Jim Gascoigne	w ret 5	Newcastle
21 Dec	Colin Foster	drew 10	Leeds

29 Dec	Arthur Burke	w pts 10	Newcastle
1931			
17 Jan	Jim Gordon	drew 10	Newcastle
18 Jan	Jackie Inwood	w pts 8	Leeds
22 Feb	Harry Stafford	w pts 10	Leeds
29 Feb	Harry Stafford	w ko 3	Hartlepool
2 Mar	George Hall	w pts 12	Newcastle
23 Mar	Wag Mosley	w ko 2	Hartlepool
25 Mar	Joe Baldasara *Featherweight compet*	w pts 3	Newcastle
25 Mar	Kid Lewis *Featherweigh compet*	w pts 3	Newcastle
18 Apr	Tommy Mason	l ret 7	Newcastle
27 Apr	Tot Murray	w pts 10	Hartlepool
4 May	Kid Seymour	w ret 5	Ashington
25 May	Young Tucker	w pts 10	Ashington
8 Jun	Alf Craster	w pts 10	Hartlepool
28 Aug	Alf Barratt	l pts 10	Glasgow
18 Sep	Willie Vint	l pts 10	Glasgow
9 Oct	Private Carter	l ret 5	Hartlepool
26 Oct	Arthur Duffy	w pts 10	Newcastle
9 Nov	Arthur Duffy	drew 10	Newcastle
23 Nov	Jim Gordon	l pts 10	Newcastle

4 Dec	Tommy Mason	w pts 10	Stockton
1932			
23 Jan	Billy Watson	l pts 10	Newcastle
12 Feb	Dave Barrie	l pts 10	Edinburgh
29 Feb	Private Carter	w rsc 1	Newcastle
19 Mar	Billy Watson	l pts 10	Stockton
21 Mar	Jim Bird	l ret 8	Newcastle
2 Apr	Billy Watson	l pts 10	Stockton
15 Apr	Eddie Donoghue	drew 10	Middlesbrough
28 May	Mickey Deans	w pts 10	West Stanley
25 Jun	Arthur Duffy	w ko 7	Chopwell
19 Sep	Jack Vickers	l dis 10	Newcastle
19 Nov	Harry Bell	w pts 10	Barnard Castle
30 Nov	Jack Vickers	w pts 10	Newcastle
1933			
9 Jan	Tommy Mason	w pts 10	Newcastle
16 Jan	Frank Markey	w pts 10	Greenock
9 Feb	Jimmy Ross	w pts 10	Newcastle
16 Feb	Jim Bird	l ret 5	Newcastle
28 Feb	Jim Teasdale	w pts 10	Newcastle
3 Mar	Jimmy Ross	w pts 10	Middlesbrough
10 Mar	Arthur Davis	l pts 10	Middlesbrough

25 Mar	Jim Bird	l pts 12	Sunderland
15 Apr	Danny Veitch	w pts 10	Sunderland
22 Apr	Joe McKenzie	l pts 12	Carlisle
26 May	Jimmy Ross	w pts 10	Middlesbrough
12 Jun	George Bunter	drew 10	Hartlepool
14 Jun	Billy Hutchinson	w pts 10	Newcastle
26 Aug	Bobby Clough	w dis 1	Sunderland
3 Sep	Jack Butler	drew 10	Middlesbrough
7 Oct	Jim Teasdale	w pts 10	Sunderland
11 Oct	Tommy Ray	w pts 10	Ryhope
6 Nov	Billy Graham	l pts 10	Newcastle
27 Nov	Joe Broughy	w pts 12	Darlington
1934			
19 Jan	Tommy Ray	w pts 10	New Seaham
22 Jan	Bob Simpkins	w ret 7	York
19 Feb	Frank McCall	w pts 12	Edinburgh
12 Mar	Tommy Ray	w pts 10	New Seaham
19 Mar	Tommy Marren	l pts 10	Newcastle
21 May	Bob Nichol	w pts 10	Newcastle
28 May	Billy Hutchinson	w rsc 5	Blyth
2 Jul	Miles Connolly	w pts 10	Hartlepool
27 Aug	Johnny Mack	l pts 10	Newcastle

10 Sep	Chuck Parker	l pts 10	Newcastle
29 Sep	Jack McKnight	w pts 10	Sunderland
13 Oct	Jim Bird	w pts 12	Sunderland
3 Nov	Jack Daley	w pts 12	Sunderland
24 Nov	Howard Powell	w pts 12	Sunderland
2 Dec	Billy Graham	drew 12	Middlesbrough
17 Dec	Johnny Mack	w pts 10	Newcastle
19 Dec	Jim Birch	w ko 4	Scarborough
29 Dec	Mick Miller	w pts 12	Sunderland
1935			
12 Jan	Dixie Cullen	w pts 12	Sunderland
21 Jan	George Bunter	l dis 7	Newcastle
28 Jan	George Bunter	drew 10	Newcastle
2 Feb	Frank Davey	w pts 12	Sunderland
11 Feb	George Rose	l pts 12	Newcastle
23 Feb	Pat Cowley	w pts 12	Sunderland
10 Mar	Ernie Roderick	l pts 12	Leeds
18 Mar	George Bunter	l pts 12	Hartlepool
31 Mar	George Leigh	l pts 15	Salford
21 Apr	Johnny Quill	drew 10	London
4 May	Tommy Marren	w ko 7	Sunderland
27 May	Dave McCleave	l pts 8	Clapton

8 Jun	Len Tiger Smith	w rsc 4	Belfast
22 Jun	Ivor Pickens	w pts 10	Sunderland
13 Jul	Syd Alridge	w rsc 5	Sunderland
10 Aug	Chuck Parker	w pts 12	Sunderland
7 Sep	Jack Moody	w ko 3	Sunderland
21 Sep	Jock Gibbons	w rtd 10	Sunderland
6 Oct	Pat Butler	w pts 10	Middlesbrough
11 Oct	Mark Cooper	w pts 12	North Shields
18 Nov	Jim Lawlor	l pts 10	Newcastle
16 Dec	Bobby Reid	w pts 10	Newcastle
1936			
4 Jan	Butcher Gascoigne	w pts 10	Sunderland
27 Jan	Mick Miller	w rtd 2	Kettering
8 Feb	Joe Warriner	w rtd 6	Sunderland
11 Mar	Jack Lord	l pts 6	Belfast
30 Mar	Ginger Sadd	l pts 12	Cambridge
16 Apr	Cock Moffitt	w rsc 8	Liverpool
14 May	Frank Hough	l dis 2	London
23 May	Hal Starkey	w pts 10	Sunderland
13 Jun	Bob Simpkins	w pts 15	Sunderland
1 Jul	Nat Franks	l pts 10	London
7 Aug	Hal Starkey	w pts 10	North Shields

17 Aug	Alban Mulrooney	l pts 10	Hartlepool
20 Sep	Jack Hyams	l pts 10	London
2 Oct	Tommy Moore *Northern Area Middleweight title*	w ko 4	North Shields
19 Oct	Tommy Martin	l pts 8	London
9 Nov	Dai Jones	l pts 10	Nottingham
7 Dec	Bob Reid	w pts 10	Darlington
16 Dec	Darkie Ellis	l rtd 4	Hull
1937			
1 Jan	Joe Duggan	l pts 10	North Shields
11 Jan	Butcher Gascoigne	w pts 10	Sutton-in-Ashfield
8 Feb	Charlie Parkin	l pts 10	Sutton-in-Ashfield
22 Mar	Charlie Parkin *Northern Area Middleweight title*	w pts 12	Sutton-in-Ashfield
1 May	Chuck Parker	l pts 12	Preston
21 June	Harry Gains	l rsc 7	London
10 Aug	Charlie Parkin *Northern Area Middleweight title*	l dis 12	Newcastle
8 Nov	Bob Simpkins	w pts 12	Newcastle
10 Dec	Bob Simpkins	w pts 10	North Shields

1938			
10 Jan	Jackie Moran	w pts 10	Newcastle
23 Jan	Bill Webster	w pts 12	Salford
31 Jan	Jack Hart	w pts 10	Newcastle
10 Mar	Butcher Gascoigne	l pts 10	Sheffield
6 May	Bert Gilroy	l rsc 6	Leith
29 May	Maurice Dennis	l pts 8	London
18 Jul	Jack Lord	l pts 10	Hartlepool
22 Sep	Ernie Roderick	l ko 2	Liverpool
3 Oct	Wally Pack	l rtd 4	London
1939			
13 Feb	Jackie Moran	w pts 10	Newcastle
13 Mar	Dick Freezer	w pts 10	Newcastle
27 Mar	Miles Connolly	w pts 10	Newcastle
23 Apr	Jack McKnight	w pts 10	Middlesbrough
19 May	Miles Connolly	w ko 4	North Shields
23 Jun	Ginger Sadd	l pts 10	North Shields
26 Jul	Yorky Bentley	l pts 10	Newcastle
25 Aug	Yorky Bentley	l pts 10	North Shields
7 Oct	Len Harrison	l rtd 5	Sunderland
21 Oct	Jack Hart	w pts 10	Sunderland
18 Nov	Bert Gilroy	l pts 10	Sunderland

1940			
3 Jan	Bert Gilroy	l rtd 6	Newcastle
14 Feb	Jim Berry	l pts 10	Newcastle
16 Mar	Sam Sproston	w rtd 4	Sunderland
13 Apr	Len Harrison	l dis 3	Sunderland
11 May	Charlie Parkin	w ko 4	Sunderland
1 Jun	George Wells	w rsc 2	Sunderland
22 Jul	Jim Laverick	l rtd 3	Newcastle
1942			
15 Jul	Pat Mulcahy	l rsc 7	Belfast
12 Sep	Jack Wright	w ko 2	Belfast
26 Sep	Pat Mulcahy	drew 8	Belfast
1947			
10 Apr	Bob McArdle	w pts 6	Newcastle

CERTIFICATE OF MERIT

"THE WATCHER'S" award for the best performance of the week goes to ROY MILLS (Sunderland) for defeating Tommy Moore (Royston) for the Northern Middle-weight Championship at North Shields

CHAPTER FIVE

TOM SMITH

Northern Area Featherweight Champion 1940-43
British Army Lightweight Champion 1944-45

In January 1968, on the evening when New St James Hall staged its last boxing match, Joe Shepherd, the matchmaker at the arena for the previous 20 years, with lifelong experience of the boxing game, was asked to name the top three North Eastern boxers who had appeared at the famous boxing venue. He replied:

> *'The late Tommy Watson would be my number one. My second choice may surprise some people but I would name Tom Smith, the Sunderland featherweight. Number three: Jack Casey, the Sunderland Assassin, who gave Len Harvey the fright of his life.'*[1]

The choice of Tom Smith in the second spot would surprise only those who had never seen him fight, for Smith was a superb boxer who was unlucky not to win a British title, although he had the consolation of winning the Northern Area featherweight championship, in 1940.

Tom Smith's dictum was 'hit and avoid being hit'. Easier said than done but Tom Smith managed it: he was quick to land with his own punches and was fast enough with the movement of his head and feet to avoid those thrown by his opponents. He was also a scrupulously clean fighter who kept well within the rules of what was allowed in the ring. He was equally considerate to opponents outside the ring and there are several stories which illustrate his generosity. For example, after Tom Smith and Frank Bonser had weighed in at one o clock on the day of their fight at the Royal Stadium, in May 1936, the Nottingham boxer asked Tom if he could suggest a quiet place where he could fill in the

TOM SMITH

time until the match in the evening. Without hesitation, Tom Smith invited Bonser to his own home, in Harrison's Buildings, and Frank gratefully accepted the offer - although he showed no favours to Smith in the ring that night, not that Tom expected any.[2]

Tom Smith was born in Sunderland's East End, on 26 September 1918, the fourth son of Patrick and Isabelle Smith. His father - known as Paddy - had fought professionally at the Star Music Hall in Sans Street before the First World War, and four of Tom's five brothers became boxers.[3] Mr Smith had built a gymnasium in the attic of his home in High Street East, where he taught his sons the skills of the game. Tom Smith's elder brother, Billy, had over 60 fights between 1924-31 and was on the verge of a championship match when he had to retire from the ring, at the age of 22, due to stomach trouble.[4] Tom Smith began by boxing for St Patrick's Boys' Club and, when he told his brother, Billy, that he wanted to turn professional, his brother replied: "*All right, it's a tough game, but if your mind is made up, I'll give you all the help and advice possible*", and he was as good as his word, acting as his brother's trainer and second throughout Tom's professional career. When he left school, Tom Smith found employment as a dockworker with the East Coast Timber Company and he was fortunate to find employers who were prepared to allow him time off to meet his training and boxing commitments. After 1945, he was employed by the National Docks Labour Board who were equally co-operative in granting him leave of absence.

Tom's first professional fight was a four rounder at Sunderland's Royal Stadium, on 29 August 1934, when he outpointed Johnny Curry from Wheatley Hill, and was paid 7/6d for his performance. Once launched in the professional ranks, Tom Smith fought 37 fights without defeat. After a victory over Hebburn's Don Patrick in his second professional bout, Smith moved up into six rounders where he drew with tough Joe Bewick from Ryhope and then embarked on a sequence of 34 wins, which included two victories over local rival Mickey O'Neill (then campaigning as Mickey Cole). After 14 fights, Smith moved up into the eight rounders for three fights and, on 31 July 1935, he outpointed Tommy Knight in his first ten round contest. The first man to put Tom Smith on the canvas was Paddy Cooney from Leeds. They met at Sunderland, on 9 October 1935, and in the ninth round Cooney caught Smith flush on the chin. Smith took a count of three and only his superb boxing skills saved him on this occasion. However, he came out for the tenth round and boxed his way to a points victory. Smith's first defeat came in his thirty-eighth contest when he met Sheffield's Walter Morton at the West Hartlepool Engineers' Club. Tom Smith was unused to open-air boxing and was out manouvered by the clever Yorkshireman. Two months later, they were rematched at North Shields when Tom Smith fought one of the best fights of his career to score a points victory over Morton. A rubber match between these two clever boxers seemed inevitable and they met at Leeds in November 1936 when Smith scored a convincing victory. The Leeds fans wanted to see more of Smith and, three weeks later, he returned to the city matched against the highly-rated Billy McHugh. This contest constituted a big step up in class for Smith but he rose to the occasion and earned a draw.

Tom Smith was now being recognised as a potential champion and Jack Cummings took over as his manager, although Billy Smith continued as his brother's trainer and cornerman. Jack Cummings was a local builder who also managed fighters. He had his office in Matamba Terrace in the Millfield area of the town. At the rear of his premises he had a builder's yard with a fully-equipped gymnasium built above his workshops. The gym was used by a number of Sunderland boxers, in the 1930's, including Tom Smith, Paddy Ross, Hughie Smith and Jack Todd, who trained and sparred with each other. Tom Smith believed strongly in gym work and he liked to spar with as many different boxers as

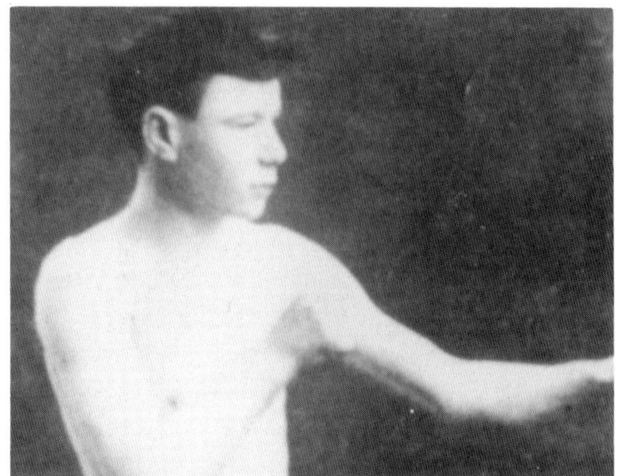

Young Billy Smith.

Billy Smith, his brother Tom's
trainer and second.

possible as part of his training programme. Tom Smith was well managed by Jack Cummings who did the job without remuneration. Tom Smith did not fight too often and he was never outmatched, meeting better class opponents and moving steadily up the rankings as his boxing talent matured.

In 1937, Smith had 14 fights, winning 11 of them and losing twice to Bobby Magee and once to Billy McHugh. In 1938, Smith was again on the winning trail, notching up six consecutive victories until he met Newcastle's Benny Sharkey, on 8 July, at North Shields.[5] It was a full house at the Albion Road Stadium, when the two boxers met over ten rounds, and although Smith was not outclassed, there was little doubt that Sharkey deserved the verdict. The pair were rematched three months later when it was a different story and there was dissension from the crowd when the referee gave the decision to Sharkey. Smith had done most of the leading throughout the fight whilst Sharkey had relied on his counter-punching to snatch the verdict.

The defeat did not prove a setback to Smith's championship hopes, however. Three months later, Smith met Johnny King, the British bantamweight champion, in a contest at 9st 12 lb and gave a brilliant display of boxing to win on points. Smith's next fight was a non-title match against the British featherweight champion, Belfast's Spider Kelly, and Smith held the Irishman to a draw. Smith then faced Spanish champion, Joe Martinez, who was disqualified in the third round for hitting below the belt. Smith was now fighting in peak form, and was matched with the new British featherweight champion, Johnny Cusick. After the contracts for the non-title fight were signed, Cusick went on holiday to the south of France, where he was badly sun-burned, and his doctor ordered a postponement of the fight with Smith, but, before a fresh date was arranged, Cusick agreed to defend his title against Nel Tarleton. This complicated matters and the British Board of Control, acting on legal advice, ruled that Cusick should first honour his contract with Smith and then meet Tarleton. So, on 4 October 1939, Tom Smith met the reigning champion, Johnny Cusick, in an over-weight fight at New St James Hall, but the fight turned out to be anything but a warm-up bout for the champion. The weight for the fight was fixed at 3lb over the featherweight limit, but Cusick came 2lb overweight and paid forfeit. Yet, in spite of giving away 4lb in weight to the champion, Smith won the bout in a convincing fashion, completely dictating the fight after the fourth round and ending the contest with a rousing tenth round.

After this defeat, Cusick had to defend his title against Liverpool's Nel Tarleton, whilst Tom Smith continued his winning ways with victories over Kid Tanner and Len Beynon, respectively the champions of British Guiana and Wales. Most people would have considered that Tom Smith had established the right to be given the next crack at the British title, but the Board of Control did not see it that way. The Board ruled that Tom Smith must fight his way through an eliminating series, and his first opponent would be Gateshead's Billy Charlton.

Billy Charlton was one of Tyneside's greatest fighters of the inter-war years. He made his ring debut at Blaydon, in 1931, and went on to fight the best in the game, including three epic contests with world featherweight champion, Freddie Miller. After these fights, the American described Billy Charlton as 'a fighter and a half'. Like Tom Smith, Billy Charlton had joined the Army on the outbreak of war, in 1939, and service food and lack of proper training had its effects on him.[6] In spite of strenuous last minute efforts in the gym, he was overweight at the weigh-in for his fight with Smith, but the contest still took place and Tom Smith rated it the hardest fight of his career. He won on points but said that his legs felt like rubber at the end of 15 gruelling rounds.[7]

DIRECTORS:
MAJOR J. BENNETT,
O.B.E., T.D., J.P., C.C. (CHAIRMAN)
JOHNNY BEST,
(MANAGING DIRECTOR)
C. H. MICKLE,
JULIUS HYAMS,
KENMURE KINNA,
F.R.I.B.A.

LIVERPOOL STADIUM

TELEGRAMS:
STADIUM, LIVERPOOL
TELEPHONE:
BANK 4816 (2 LINES)
SECRETARY:
GORDON GUILD,
A.B.A.

The Featherweight Championship of Gt. Britain and British Empire

FIFTEEN 3-Min. Rounds Contest at 9 stone.

NEL TARLETON

(Liverpool)
Official Featherweight Champion

versus

Sgt. TOM SMITH

(Sunderland)
Official Challenger for the above Title.

Saturday, November 2nd, 1940, at 3-30 p.m.

OFFICIAL PROGRAMME THREE PENCE

The next stage of the elimination process was a match between Tom Smith and Frank Parkes of Nottingham for the vacant Northern Area featherweight title, which was staged at New St James Hall, on 28 February 1940. For the first ten rounds, Smith allowed Parkes to do most of the forcing whilst keeping a narrow points lead, then in the last five rounds, as Parkes tired, Smith cut loose and piled up the points. Although Tom Smith was not in top form, his tactical skill and clever boxing made him a clear winner.

A month before the Smith-Parkes contest, Nel Tarleton had defeated Johnny Cusick to regain the British title, but the war upset many plans. Tom Smith joined the Durham Light Infantry, in September 1939, but he was able to continue boxing. After his Northern Area title fight, he fought Frank Kenny, at Newcastle, and on 6 April 1940, he met Frank Keery on a war-time charity bill at Sunderland's Victoria Hall. A fortnight later, he was posted to France, stopping off in London en route to outpoint Jackie Rankin over ten rounds at Earls Court.

Tom Smith's regiment was caught up in the German attack on the Low Countries, in May 1940, and Tom Smith was one of 300,000 Allied troops who were evacuated from the Dunkirk beaches, between 26 May and 4 June. Back in Britain, Smith was involved in his regiment's regrouping and preparations for the expected German invasion, and he received rapid promotion to the rank of sergeant. Almost all sporting activities were suspended during the Battle of Britain, July- September 1940, but in October the British Boxing Board announced that Tom Smith should meet Nel Tarleton for the British and Empire featherweight titles.[8]

The champion, Tarleton, was numbered by Gilbert Odd among British boxing's all-time greats.[9] In all, Tarleton took part in ten British championship contests, winning the title three times in the process. No other British champion ever twice lost his crown in the ring and twice regained it. Tarleton retired in 1947 as the proud owner of two Lonsdale Belts. He was tall for a featherweight with a long reach which he knew how to use to best advantage and was a skilful and ringwise boxer.

Tom Smith spars with young Hughie Smith during preparations for his championship fight with Nel Tarleton in 1940.

The fight was fixed to take place at Liverpool Stadium on the afternoon of Saturday 2 November 1940. The title match had come as a complete surprise to Tom Smith and it found him undertrained and overweight. He was granted two weeks special leave to prepare for the fight and trained in the Matamba Terrace gym, in Sunderland, breaking off training two days before the match to enjoy a couple of days of light training and relaxation, at Southport.

The air raid sirens sounded during the bout and the referee, Moss Dejong, indicated that the fight would continue, and the spectators remained in their seats as the bombs rained down on Merseyside. The contest, somewhat overshadowed by the dramatic events taking place outside, was a fight between two evenly matched boxers and it ended with a narrow points victory for Tarleton. Some observers believed that if Smith had forced the pace from the opening bell, he could have worn down his older opponent. Instead, he chose to box Tarleton and this suited the old fox who was able to pace himself over the 15 rounds.

A couple of months later, Smith outpointed Edinburgh's Jimmy Watson, at New St James Hall, and after the fight Smith's manager, Jack Cummings, raised the question of a return match between Smith and Tarleton with Fred Charlton, matchmaker at the Hall. His reply was: '*Yes, but we cannot contact Nel*'. Apparently Tarleton, who was then serving in the RAF had been posted to the Orkneys, but when he heard of the proposals he readily agreed to an overweight match with Tom Smith. '*It's damned lonesome up here,* 'joked Nel, '*and a fight engagement is the only way I can get a few days leave.*'[10]

The pair duly met at New St James Hall, on 5 February 1941, over ten rounds and, at the end of the bout, the referee, Eugene Henderson, had no hesitation in raising Smith's hand.

Sunderland Ex-Boxers' Association.
left to right : Jack Casey, Tom Smith and Danny Veitch

Whilst waiting for another shot at Tarleton's title, Smith picked up what fights he could. On 28 March 1941, he knocked out Glasgow's Don Cameron in the first round at Newcastle, and three months later he travelled down to London to meet Johnny Ward at the Royal Albert Hall. Ward, from Roscommon, had the reputation of being a slugger and he was half a stone overweight at the weigh-in, whereupon Smith's handlers exclaimed: 'No fight!' However, Tom Smith was put under heavy pressure to enter the ring against the Irishman to 'save the bill' and he gave in. Ward was determined to use his weight advantage and he flung wild punches at Smith from the opening bell until the third round, when he was disqualified for hitting below the belt. Smith followed up with three fights at New St James Hall, defeating Warren Kendall on points, Billy Charlton - who retired with a cut eye in the sixth round - and Jackie Rankin on points. The Boxing Board then matched him with Dundee's Jim Brady in an eliminating bout for a British title fight and this contest took place at Leeds, on 24 November 1941. For some reason the 'big money' at the ringside was on Brady but Tom Smith turned in one of his most polished performances to win on points over 12 rounds. Once again, he had established himself as the official number one contender for Tarleton's title.

In 1942, Tom Smith was remustered to the Army Physical Training Corps and his new job took him all over the country. He was no longer settled in the DLI depot, in County Durham, where he could combine a regular training programme with his military duties. Consequently, he had only three fights in 1942. On 5 February, he outpointed Dave Crowley, former British lightweight champion, over 10 rounds at New St James Hall, and in August he outpointed Jackie Rankin, his most persistent opponent, over 10 rounds at London's Queensberry Club. Then, on 28 September, he faced Ronnie James, the Welsh lightweight champion and the leading contender for the British title, at the Queensberry Club. In tackling James, Smith was giving away weight to a top class opponent and, although he turned in a plucky performance, he was forced to retire in the sixth round. Tom Smith could not cope with James's barrage of heavy punches and this was the only time in his career that he was stopped inside the distance.

In 1943, Tom Smith relinquished his Northern Area featherweight title because he felt he was in no position to defend it, and over the next two years he took part only in service tournaments and exhibition bouts. On 8 March 1944, he defeated Gunner L.Malone over three rounds, at Blackpool, to win the British Army's lightweight title and retained the title the following year when he defeated Bdr.C.Fox at Manchester. On 13 May 1945, he outpointed Aircraftman J Rankin of the RAF in an inter-service tournament, at Antwerp, the only time he ever boxed on foreign soil.

He returned to the professional ring, on 17 July 1945, when he outpointed Dave Crowley over eight rounds at White Hart Lane on the undercard of the Jack London - Bruce Woodcock British and Empire heavyweight title fight. In the following month, he drew the crowds to Roker Park where he topped the bill against Kid Tanner. Smith weighed in at 9st 3lb suggesting that, with a return to a rigorous training schedule and a controlled diet, he could still make the featherweight limit. In the Army bouts, he had fought as a lightweight and some boxing commentators believed that he would move up into this class when he resumed professional boxing, but this did not prove to be the case. In his fight with Tanner, he demonstrated that he had lost none of his old skills, although the fight was marred by Tanner's tendency to hold. In his last fight of the year, he beat Dave Finn at the Queensberry Club.

In January 1946, Sergeant Smith was demobilised and returned to his former job on the Sunderland docks. Back in his old training routines, he picked up the threads of his boxing career and, in July, he outpointed Jarrow's Ben Duffy, in a ten round bout staged at the South Shields Greyhound Stadium, and two months later he outpointed Ronnie Clayton over ten rounds at Leeds.

He was boxing as well as he had ever done and he needed to be in top form for his next fight when he was matched with Ray Famechon, the French featherweight, at the Royal Albert Hall. Famechon was a first class boxer who went on to win the European title and to fight Willie Pep for the world championship. Like Smith, he was a clever ringmaster and the pair served up eight rounds of the 'sweet science' before the decision was awarded to Smith. It was a close decision but widely held to have been the correct one and the referee told Smith that his clean punching had tipped the balance in his favour. Looking back, after his retirement from the ring, Smith declared the Frenchman to have been 'the best featherweight I ever fought.'[11]

Smith had to put himself on a starvation diet in order to make the weight and there was an amusing incident at the weigh-in when a boxing official asked Smith:

> *'Are you Famechon?'*
> *'Famishin'? I'll say I am,' replied Smith, 'I haven't had a solid meal for three days.'*[12]

A week later, Tom Smith lost on points over eight rounds to Swansea's Cliff Curvis, at Harringay, on the night that Joe Baksi stopped Freddie Mills in six rounds. However, he ended the year with wins over Danny Woods and Paddy Dowdell.

In February 1947, Nel Tarleton relinquished the British featherweight title and the Board of Control ruled that Ronnie Clayton must meet Joe Carter, in the first stage of an elimination process, the winner of this bout would meet Tom Smith, and the winner of Tom Smith's contest would fight Al Phillips, the

'Aldgate tiger', for the vacant title. On 27 March 1947, Clayton knocked out Carter in the fifth round, and Tom Smith kept busy by outpointing Paddy Dowdell and Gerry Smyth. There was some delay in arranging a Clayton - Smith bout, although it looked as though the fight would be staged at Roker Park, when Tom Smith announced, on 28 May, that he could no longer make the 9 stone weight. He added that he would continue his boxing career as a lightweight.

His manager, Jack Cummings, announced: 'He will go in at the top', and Smith's first opponent in the heavier class was to be Andre Famechon, brother of Ray and a leading French lightweight. Cummings said that the aim was for Smith to defeat Famechon and then challenge the winner of the Stan Hawthorne - Billy Thompson bout. The Hawthorne - Thompson fight had been arranged for the following month to decide who would succeed Ronnie James as the British lightweight champion. Cummings' plans did not work out, however, for Smith lost on points to the Frenchman.

Smith weighed in at 9st 9lb as a fully-fledged lightweight and he started strongly, taking the first few rounds, but then Famechon came more into the fight and he ended with a grandstand finish in the tenth round. After the fight, Famechon said that he would be glad to leave austerity Britain with its strict food rationing and return to France to have a good meal.

Although Smith had lost on points to Famechon, he was by no means out-classed by the Frenchman and, at the age of 29, he appeared to have several good years still ahead of him, with the possibility of earning some big money in the post-war boxing boom. Therefore, it came as a surprise when he announced his retirement from boxing, on 24 September 1947. Tom Smith explained that he could no longer regulate his weight: he could reduce his weight by several pounds one day only to find that it had gone up on the next day. He did not want to jeopardise his health by a constant battle with the scales and had therefore decided to retire.

As a docker, Tom Smith took a keen interest in the National Dock Labour Board's boxing tournaments and he coached some of the local lads who entered the Board's competitions. He never lost his interest in the boxing scene and became a very popular President of the Sunderland Ex-Boxers' Association. He looked back upon his boxing career with modesty and humour. When someone once asked him what had been his greatest fight, he replied with a twinkle in his eye: 'The first one - I got paid 7/6d for it'[13]. His other sporting interest which he shared with his son, Colin, was watching football. His daughter, Ann, married Leslie Quenet who had a very impressive record as an amateur boxer with Lambton Street Boys' Club and a short - and promising - spell under the name Les Darnell in the professional ranks, 1949-51. Tom Smith died on 14 April 1990, at the age of 71, and a requiem mass was held at St Joseph's Church, Millfield, not far from the gymnasium where he had trained during his boxing career.

CERTIFICATE OF MERIT

"BOXING'S" Award for the best performance of the week goes to TOM SMITH (Sunderland) for his points victory over John Cusick, the British and Empire Feather-weight Champion, over 10 rounds at Newcastle on October 4, 1939

BOXING Phone 2552
ROYAL STADIUM, SUNDERLAND
WEDNESDAY—7.30
Great Return Contest
TOM SMITH v. PAT MURPHY
(Undefeated) (Jarrow)
Ten Rounds
DAVE GORDON v. BILLY GORDON
OTHER CONTESTS
Prices: 3d, 6d, 9d.

FIRST-CLASS BOXING!
VICTORIA HALL, SUNDERLAND
SATURDAY, APRIL 6, at 7 o'clock
(In aid of the Mayor's War Fund)
TEN THREE-MINUTE ROUNDS
Pte. TOM SMITH
(Sunderland), Northern Champion
v.
JIM KEERY
(Lisburn), Ireland's Best Featherweight
JACK TODD v. BOB HENRY.
PTE. PADDY GILL v. IKE PRATT
OTHER CONTESTS.
Admission 1/-, 2/-, 3/6 (bookable). Tickets to all parts on sale at Pompa's.

New
St. JAMES'S HALL
NEWCASTLE-ON-TYNE
BOXING! Thursday,
June 19th — 6.45.
TOM SMITH
Sunderland's Title Contender
v.
ANDRE FAMECHON
French Title Contender
£1/1/- Reserved, 10/6, 6/-,
Pay at Door.

TOM SMITH'S RING RECORD 1934-47

1934			
29 Aug	Johnny Curry	w pts 4	Sunderland
15 Sep	Don Patrick	w pts 6	Sunderland
6 Oct	Joe Berwicke	drew 6	Sunderland
3 Nov	Billy Lawson	w pts 6	Sunderland
24 Nov	Mickey O'Neill(Cole)	w pts 6	Sunderland
5 Dec	Harry Dent	w pts 6	York
22 Dec	Young Conn	w ko 2	Sunderland
1935			
19 Jan	Mickey O'Neill(Cole)	w dis 2	Sunderland
2 Feb	Jack Finn	w pts 6	Sunderland
23 Feb	Jack Hill	w rsc 2	Sunderland
9 Mar	Bob Hendry	w pts 6	Sunderland
13 Apr	Mickey O'Neill	w pts 6	Sunderland
3 May	Curly Dunn	w dis 1	Middlesbrough
11 May	Charlie Curry	w pts 6 w	Sunderland
19 May	Curly Dunn	w rsc 4	Middlesbrough
1 Jun	George Johnson	w pts 8	Sunderland
3 Jul	Pat Murphy	w pts 8	Sunderland
17 Jul	Pat Murphy	w pts 8	Sunderland
31 Jul	Tommy Knight	w pts 10	Sunderland

28 Aug	Johnny Donnelly	w pts 10	Sunderland
18 Sep	Pat Murphy	w ret 8	Sunderland
29 Sep	Harry Brooks	w pts 10	Middlesbrough
9 Oct	Paddy Cooney	w pts 10	Sunderland
30 Oct	Johnny Butler	w pts 10	Sunderland
20 Nov	Ronnie Lewis	w pts 10	Sunderland
4 Dec	Frank Walker	w pts 10	Sunderland
21 Dec	Joe Rolfe	w rsc 10	Sunderland
1936			
15 Jan	Jim O'Neill	w pts 10	Sunderland
5 Feb	Johnny Lynch	w pts 10	Sunderland
14 Feb	Tommy Knight	w rsc 9	North Shields
24 Feb	Les Brown	w pts 10	Darlington
29 Feb	Charlie Reed	w pts 10	Sunderland
21 Mar	Nipper Carroll	w pts 10	Sunderland
3 Apr	Les Brown	w rsc 7	North Shields
11 Apr	Joey Jacobs	w ret 7	Sunderland
5 May	Kid Rich	w pts 10	Sunderland
16 May	Frank Bonser	w pts 10	Sunderland
6 Jun	Jim Hayes	w pts 10	Sunderland
15 Jun	Walter Morton	l pts 10	Hartlepool
28 Jul	Kid Rich	w dis 3	Middlesbrough

21 Aug	Walter Morton	w pts 10	North Shields
11 Sep	Tommy Tune	w pts 10	North Shields
16 Oct	Jim Whitworth	w ko 4	Sunderland
1 Nov	Walter Morton	w pts 10	Leeds
20 Nov	Tommy Atherton	w rsc 6	North Shields
27 Nov	Billy McHugh	drew 12	Leeds
4 Dec	Vinney Elliott	w pts 10	North Shields
1937			
22 Jan	Bobby Magee	l pts 12	North Shields
6 Feb	Kid Saxby	w pts 12	Sunderland
26 Feb	Ginger Lawson	w pts 10	Newcastle
20 Mar	Pat Nugent	w pts 10	Sunderland
3 Apr	Frank Finney	w rsc 7	Sunderland
4 Jun	Johnny Regan	w pts 10	North Shields
25 Jun	Ginger Lawson	w pts 10	North Shields
16 Jul	Billy McHugh	l pts 12	North Shields
6 Aug	Ted Green	w pts 12	North Shields
3 Sep	Joe Mullings	w rsc 5	North Shields
14 Sep	Ike Pratt	w pts 12	Newcastle
24 Sep	Syd Parker	w pts 12	North Shields
12 Nov	Harold Naylor	w ret 3	North Shields
17 Dec	Bobby Magee	l pts 12	North Shields

1938			
31 Jan	Johnny Jones	w pts 10	Newcastle
18 Feb	Tommy Miller	w ko 2	North Shields
1 Apr	Joe Thompson	w pts 10	North Shields
22 Apr	Joe Thompson	w pts 10	North Shields
29 Apr	George Smith	w pts 10	North Shields
10 Jun	George Smith	w pts 10	North Shields
8 Jul	Benny Sharkey	l pts 10	North Shields
12 Aug	George Marsden	w pts 10	North Shields
2 Sep	Norman Denny	w pts 10	North Shields
14 Oct	Benny Sharkey	l pts 10	North Shields
14 Nov	Jake Carr	w pts 12	Newcastle
1939			
16 Jan	Johnny King	w pts 10	Newcastle
13 Mar	Spider Kelly	drew 10	Newcastle
24 Apr	Joe Martinez	w dis 3	Newcastle
7 Jul	Johnny Walker	w pts 10	North Shields
4 Oct	Johnny Cusick	w pts 10	Newcastle
1 Nov	Kid Tanner	w pts 10	Newcastle
29 Nov	Len Beynon	w pts 10	Newcastle
27 Dec	Billy Charlton	w pts 15	Newcastle

1940			
17 Jan	Jimmy Watson	w rsc 10	Newcastle
7 Feb	Dick Corbett	w pts 10	Hartlepool
28 Feb	Frank Parkes *Northern Area Featherweight title*	w pts 15	Newcastle
27 Mar	Frank Kenny	w rsc 2	Newcastle
6 Apr	Jim Keery	w pts 10	Sunderland
22 Apr	Jackie Rankin	w pts 10	London
2 Nov	Nel Tarleton *British and Empire Featherweight title*	l pts 15	Liverpool
1941			
1 Jan	Jimmy Watson	w pts 10	Newcastle
5 Feb	Nel Tarleton	w pts 10	Newcastle
28 May	Don Cameron	w ko 1	Newcastle
12 Jun	Johnny Ward	w dis 3	London
27 Aug	Warren Kendall	w pts 10	Newcastle
17 Sep	Billy Charlton	w ret 5	Newcastle
1 Oct	Jackie Rankin	w pts 10	Newcastle
24 Nov	Jim Brady	w pts 12	Leeds
1942			
5 Feb	Dave Crowley	w pts 10	Newcastle
27 Aug	Jackie Rankin	w pts 8	London

23 Sep	Ronnie James	l rsc 6	London
1944			
8 Mar	Gunner L Malone *British Army* *Lightweight title*	w pts 3	Blackpool
1945			
29 Mar	Bombardier C Fox *British Army* *Lightweight title*	w pts 3	Manchester
17 Jul	Dave Crowley	w pts 8	London
4 Aug	Kid Tanner	w pts 10	Sunderland
16 Oct	Dave Finn	w pts 8	London
1946			
18 Jul	Ben Duffy	w pts 10	South Shields
10 Sep	Ronnie Clayton	w pts 10	Leeds
28 Oct	Ray Famechon	w pts 8	London
5 Nov	Cliff Curvis	l pts 8	London
14 Nov	Danny Woods	w rsc 6	Newcastle
12 Dec	Paddy Dowdall	w pts 8	Newcastle
1947			
14 Apr	Paddy Dowdall	w pts 10	Leeds
24 Apr	Gerry Smyth	w pts 8	Newcastle
19 Jun	Andre Famechon	l pts 8	Newcastle

CHAPTER SIX

HUGHIE SMITH

Northern Area Lightweight Champion 1949-51

Hughie Smith was a schoolboy boxer who won his first tournament at the age of 12. He joined the professional ranks, in 1939, won the Northern Area lightweight title, in 1949, and fought his last professional bout, at the Motor City Arena, Detroit, in 1951. Like other sportsmen of his generation, the war years cut a swathe through his career, but hc was well placed to take part in Britain's post-war boxing boom and seized the chance of winning an area title. Smith was a promoter's fighter: he had a two-handed attacking style which pleased the crowds and he was prepared to fight anywhere, often at short notice. His career was shrewdly managed by Jack McBeth, who had been matchmaker at the Sunderland Royal and the North Shields' Albion Road stadiums, in the 1930's. Hughie was not related to Tom Smith, although they trained in the same gym, and Hughie Smith was always grateful for the sound advice he received from his more experienced namesake.

Hughie Smith was born in the Southwick area of Sunderland, on 5 October 1923, the son of James and Philomena Smith. Like many other fighters, he had some Irish blood in his veins: his maternal grandfather, Hugh McDermott, was born in Donegal and had worked in Scotland before moving down to Sunderland where he was employed as a holder-on in the shipyards. Hughie was educated at St Hilda's School in Southwick and he became interested in boxing through the school.

In 1935, he won his first boxing tournament, promoted by Father Cahill of St Mary's Church. Father Cahill was a parish priest who had organised a Catholic Youth Association in the town, based at

HUGHIE SMITH

St Mary's Youth Club, in Matlock Street, which included boxing among its activities. The club's gymnasium was actually located in a former public house. Two other famous Sunderland fighters of the 1930's, Paddy Gill and Mickey O'Neill (real name Gill and, in fact, Paddy's brother) had started as amateur boxers, at St. Mary's Youth Club. Father Cahill's tournament was open to pupils from all Catholic schools in the town and Hughie Smith represented St Hilda's in the 4st 7lb class. The bouts were held at the Royal Stadium in Bedford Street, and the 12 year old Hughie Smith emerged as the winner at his weight. From then on he wanted to be a boxer and although continuing to fight as an amateur he was impatient to reach the age of 16 when he would become old enough to register with the B.B. of C. as a professional boxer.

At 14, he left school and worked as a catcher at Pickersgill's shipyard, and then served his time as a plater at Clark's. He also began to train at Jack Cumming's gym, in Matamba Terrace, Millfield, where he had the benefit of training with Tom Smith. "*It was there I learned the value of physical fitness and self discipline*", recalled Hughie. "*Tom Smith insisted that peak fitness was number one priority and I never forgot his advice.*"

Hughie Smith's first four professional fights were at the Pottery Buildings, in Sunderland's East End, for which he received 15/- a bout. One of his earliest opponents, whom he met on a war-time charity bill at Sunderland's Victoria Hall, was Jackie 'Kid' Horseman from West Hartlepool, like Smith a future Northern Area champion. Smith held Horseman in great respect: "*You could never tell where Jackie's punches were coming from. He would suddenly catch you with a swinging right hand punch. My own strong suit was stamina, but Jackie had plenty too.*"

Hughie's first manager was local builder, Jack Cummings, before Jack McBeth took charge of his affairs. There were few promotions during the war years but Jack McBeth was able to fix up a few fights, mainly on charity bills. In 1944, Hughie Smith volunteered for the RAF and was enrolled as a trainee air gunner, but after a three month reception course, at Scarborough, he was drafted back to the shipyards with reserved occupation status.

He had no fights from July 1943 until November 1944, when he was approached by Jack McBeth with the offer of a ten round contest with Tommy Miller, in Glasgow. Smith was fit enough but he had never fought ten rounds before and feared that he would be ring-rusty after his long lay-off. However, the purse offer was a tempting £5 plus expenses and he agreed to the match. The venue was the Grove Stadium in the Anderton district of the city. Smith remembers that the stadium was a converted church, with the ring standing where the altar had been and the spectators sitting in the former nave. The dressing rooms were in a crypt below the church and the contestants entered the arena from below. Tommy Miller was a popular local fighter, but Smith recalls that he got a good reception from the sporting Scottish crowd when he entered the ring. In spite of his eighteen month absence from the ring, Smith turned in one of his best performances. He carried the fight to Miller and took a lot of punishment in doing so, being badly cut about the eyes, but his aggression paid off in the ninth round when he landed a knock-out blow.

On 24 November 1944, Hughie Smith was matched with Cyril Maudsley, at the Tower Circus Arena, in Blackpool. This meant a weary war-time rail journey for Hughie, changing trains at York and Manchester, and he turned up at the stadium after 7pm. When he arrived, the promoter, Johnny Best, grumbled: "*I'm paying you lads good money, the least you can do is get here on time.*" Hughie was rushed through his medical and weigh-in, and then pitched into the ring against Maudsley who was putting together a good run of victories at this time. Hughie held his own in the

Danny Veitch checks Hughie Smith's gloves before an open air contest at Roker Park on 4 August 1945.

early rounds but Maudsley caught him with a barrage of punches, in the fifth round, and the referee intervened to stop the fight. Hughie Smith was back at the same venue in the following month when he stopped Harry Barrett in the third round.

Ten weeks later, Smith was back at the Grove, in Glasgow, matched against the experienced and hard-hitting Johnny Smith from Clydesbank. For this fight, Hughie Smith was paid a purse of £10, his biggest to date. The two Smiths made it an exciting toe-to-toe slugging match and, at the end of ten rounds, the decision was awarded to Johnny Smith on points. They were rematched, a fortnight later, when it was a repeat performance, until the ninth round, when Johnny Smith landed a big punch which put Hughie down. He rose at the count of nine, ready to continue - and still insists that he beat the count - but the referee ruled that he was out on his feet and the decision was registered as a knock-out.

Hughie Smith was philosophical about referees' decisions. Many of his fights were away from Wearside against boxers who had the support of a home crowd, and Smith believed that if a decision was very close, the home town boxer would be given the benefit of the doubt. He regarded this as a fact of life and did not feel bitter about it.

One of the few referees' decisions which rankled with him was when he lost to Johnny Fitzpatrick, at New St James Hall, on 30 January 1947. Fitzpatrick was from Bruce Woodcock's Doncaster school of boxing and he and Hughie Smith had drawn a bout, in Derby, fourteen months earlier. When they met, at Newcastle, Hughie Smith was well on top. He had Fitzpatrick down for an early count of nine and, in the sixth round, the Wearsider landed a left hook to the body which dropped Fitzpatrick again. The referee began his count and reached eight, while there were shouts of : 'Foul!' and 'Low blow!' coming from Fitzpatrick's corner.

The referee then stopped counting and told Smith that he was disqualified. Hughie Smith felt that he was on the wrong end of some bad refereeing and he was, of course, fined by the Boxing Board of Control for the alleged offence. The two men were rematched at Doncaster Corn Exchange eighteen months later when Hughie knocked out Fitzpatrick with a right blow to the body in the third round. Fitzpatrick asked for a fourth match and the pair duly met at the Farrar Street stadium, Middlesbrough, on 17 January 1949. Smith charged out of his corner at the opening bell and put Fitzpatrick down three times with body punches before delivering the knock-out blow. This decisive first round victory over the Yorkshireman settled beyond doubt who was the better man and it undoubtedly helped to get Hughie Smith his crack at the Northern Area title, later in the year.

After the end of the war, Hughie Smith took a labouring job on a building site. The heavy manual work fitted in well with his training programme, and his employer was prepared to allow him the time off to box. Over the three year period, 1945-47, he had 33 fights and was meeting good class fighters such as Jimmy Jury and Dick Levers. In 1948, he lost on points to master boxer, George Daly, then nearing the end of his boxing career, at the Grange Road Baths, Bermondsey; and he was out-pointed by another good London boxer, Tommy Barnham, who went on to win the Southern Area title. Smith was paid £60 for meeting Barnham at the Lime Grove Baths, Shepherds Bush, a good purse for that time. Both Daly and Barnham were rated among Britain's top ten lightweights, in 1948.

Hughie continued to pick up fights, in 1949, and in May stood in as a late substitute against Gerry Smyth of Belfast, a future Northern Ireland title holder, at Dunmore Park. Two months later, he was again a last minute substitute, this time against Allan Tanner of British Guiana, at Liverpool. The fight was stopped in the second round when Smith sustained a badly cut eye. Allan

Tanner was the younger brother of the famous Kid Tanner and Hughie Smith rated him highly among the opponents he met in the ring.

Then, in August 1949, after ten years in the professional ranks, Hughie was matched with Jimmy Trotter of Shildon for the vacant Northern Area lightweight title. Trotter, a fitter at the Shildon railway workshops, was a former member of the English amateur boxing team, who had turned professional the previous year at the late age of 27. The fight was to be an open-air contest, held at the Hendon cricket ground, on 17 August 1949. At the afternoon weigh-in, Trotter had difficulty in making the weight and he had to go on the scales twice to meet the 9st 9lb limit. Hughie Smith was a comfortable 1oz within the weight limit at the first attempt. It was a warm, pleasant evening and a crowd of 2000 turned up to watch the fight. Smith had the advantage of fighting before a home crowd, but Shildon was only twenty miles away and there was a fair sprinkling of Trotter's supporters among the spectators.

Jimmy Trotter was much taller than Smith, and it was obvious that he would want to keep the fight at long range, whereas Smith would be trying to slip Trotter's left leads and move in close. The opening round was a quiet one as both men felt each other out, but in the second and third rounds Smith opened up and landed some good body punches. Trotter recovered in the fourth and he caught Smith with a couple of good right hand punches, but failed to follow up. The fifth round also went to Trotter who scored with his long left hand. Smith pinned Trotter on the ropes with some good body punching, in the seventh round. The fight see-sawed between the two men until the last two rounds, when Smith showed greater stamina and he finished both rounds with strong two-handed rallies. It was enough to win him the fight and the Northern Area lightweight championship.

In October, Smith met Les Randle of Hull, over eight rounds, at the Farrar Street Stadium. Middlesbrough, in what was described as 'one of the hardest fights ever seen in this arena.' It was an all-action bout which Smith lost on points. A month later, Smith stopped Harry Brown of Derby in the fourth round, when Brown retired with a cut eye.

Scotland had a good crop of lightweights, in the early '50's, and Hughie Smith - always welcome in Scottish rings - was matched against the best of them, in 1950. In January, he lost on points to Jim Findlay and, in March, to Johnny Flannigan, both men being future Scottish champions. In July, he met Harry Hughes, the reigning Scottish champion, at Coatbridge, and lost narrowly on points. The two men were rematched, the following month, when the result was the same.

Scottish lightweight champion, Harry Hughes,
holds with his right as Hughie Smith bores
in on him, at Coatbridge on 19 July 1950

Although Hughie lost these four fights on points, he did so by narrow margins. When he fought the former ABA champion, Algar Smith, at the Albert Hall, in April, however, Hughie Smith boxed below his best and the referee stopped the fight in the third of a six round contest. The Smith v Smith bout was part of the undercard to the top of the bill light heavyweight contest between Don Cockell and Jimmy Carroll.

Hughie set off for London, on the day of the fight, on a train which should have got him there in plenty of time for the weigh-in, at Jack Solomon's gym, in Great Windmill Street, Soho. Unfortunately, the train was held up at Grantham and Hughie was too late for the weigh-in, and Nat Sellers had to arrange a late weigh-in for him. The uncertainty and rushing about was not the best preparation for the fight against Algar Smith and Hughie paid the price in the ring that night. Algar, a fighter from an Essex gypsy family, was unbeaten since turning professional in the previous year, and his boxing career was being skilfully managed by his London handlers. Algar Smith caught Hughie against the ropes in the third round and, when the Wearsider sank to his knees to take a count, the referee stepped in and stopped the fight. Hughie felt that he could have carried on and recovered from a shaky start but the referee did not give him the chance.

In the same year, the Northern Area Council of the British Boxing Board ruled that Jimmy Trotter should meet Bob Hodgson, a Seaham miner, in an eliminating contest, the winner to meet Hughie Smith for the Northern Area title. Trotter and Hodgson duly met, at Ryhope, in July, when Hodgson won in the eighth round. Hughie Smith was at the fight to run the rule over his future opponent, but in the event Hodgson and Smith never met in the ring. In 1951, after fights against Charlie Wisdom and Tony McTigue, Hughie Smith emigrated to Canada and relinquished the Northern Area title. Bob Hodgson never got a championship match, and the Northern Area lightweight title remained vacant, until March 1990, when it was won by Tyneside's Paul Charters.

Hughie Smith worked for Labatt's brewery, in London, Ontario, and was soon in action in the Canadian ring. In July 1951, he fought Remo Odiroco, a Canadian of Italian parentage, at the local stadium, and stopped him in four rounds. Three months later, he crossed the border to meet Eddie Nelson of Grand Rapids at the Motor City Arena, Detroit. Smith was doing well until the third round when a cut eye prompted the referee to stop the fight. One of the spectators at the fight was Jake La Motta, the former world middleweight champion, who came round to the dressing rooms to chat to Hughie Smith after the contest. The Bronx Bull was interested to learn what he could about Randolph Turpin who had just lost the world middleweight title to Sugar Ray Robinson. Another visitor to Hughie's dressing room that night was Arthur Tracey, the former Preston welterweight who had emigrated to America in the 1930's, where he became a manager.

"How's Jack Casey getting along?" he wanted to know, and after being told that Casey was still alive, he commented: *"I was never lucky enough to see Jack Casey in action but I read a lot about him. He would have made a packet in the U.S.A."*

The Detroit fight was the last of Hughie Smith's boxing career. He could have had more fight engagements, but found it difficult to fit these in with his job at Labatt's and, with a growing family, his work at the brewery had to come first. If it had been possible to make suitable arrangements, then Hughie Smith could have been launched on a new boxing career, in North America, although, as he says, he was then 28 years old and had been boxing since he was a boy and it was a good time to retire from the ring.

The Smith family stayed in Canada for eight years and two of Hughie's five children were born there, but the pull of England proved too strong and they came back to Sunderland, in 1959. Hughie found employment with an engineering firm, on the Southwick Trading Estate, where he worked until his retirement.

Hughie Smith became a member of the Sunderland Ex-Boxers Association and, in 1974, they arranged a social evening in his honour at the Southwick Social Club, which was attended by several of his former ring opponents. Hughie has always been a strong family man and he takes great pleasure in the progress of his grandchildren. He says he enjoyed every minute of his time in the ring and his only regret is that he is now too old to put on the gloves and go a few rounds.

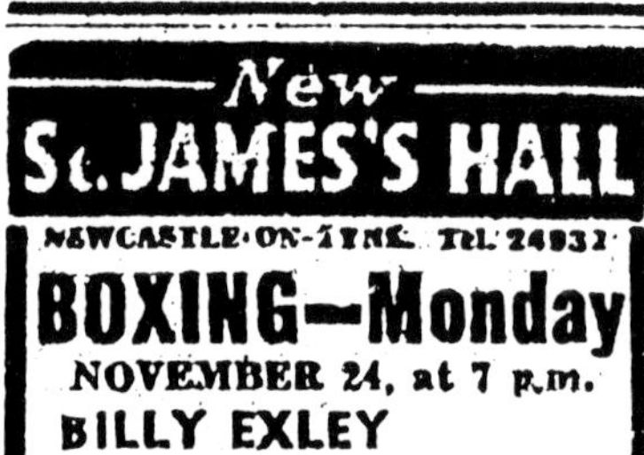

BOXING

RYHOPE BOYS' CLUB GROUNDS

To-morrow, May 22, at 3 p.m.

Promoter Fred Simm, B.B.B. of C., presents:

HUGH SMITH, Sunderland, v.
DICK LEVERS, Chesterfield.

Bert Ingram, Ryhope, v.
George Casson, North Shields.

Three Grand Supporting Contests.

Ringside 3/- Area 1/6

Buses and trains stop two minutes from arena.

Cycle park for 500 with attendance.

BOXING

TO-NIGHT AT 7.15

HENDON CRICKET GROUND

Northern Area Light-weight Championship

12 Three-minute Rounds.

HUGH SMITH (Sunderland) v.
JIMMY TROTTER (Shildon)

BOB TAYLOR (Blackhall Mill)
v. JOE CARR (South Shields)

3 Strong Supporting Contests.

Ringside 4/- Boys 2/- Area 2/-
Boys 1/-

HUGHIE SMITH'S RING RECORD 1939-51

1939			
14 Oct	Joe Peters	l pts 6	Sunderland
28 Oct	Bob Haynes	w ko 4	Sunderland
1940			
13 Jan	Kid Brown	w ko 3	Sunderland
30 Mar	Jim Evans	w ko 3	Sunderland
6 Apr	Jackie Horseman	w pts 8	Sunderland
1 May	Freddie Farrell	l pts 6	Newcastle
8 Sep	Seaman Ray (R. Navy)	w rsc 2	Middlesbrough
12 Oct	Jack Todd	l dis 3	Newcastle
26 Dec	L/Cpl Higson(R.N.F.)	l rsc 2	Newcastle
1941			
12 Feb	Cpl. Jones(R.A.F.)	l pts 6	Newcastle
25 Jul	Jack Todd	w ko 2	South Shields
27 Aug	Terry McGovern	w rsc 3	Newcastle
1943			
3 Apr	Deb Seaton	w rsc 3	Sunderland
12 Jul	Billy Hanson	w pts 8	Sunderland
1944			
4 Nov	Tommy Miller	w ko 9	Glasgow
24 Nov	Cyril Maudsley	l rsc 5	Blackpool

29 Dec	Harry Barrett	w rsc 3	Blackpool
1945			
10 Mar	Johnny Smith	l pts 10	Glasgow
24 Mar	Johnny Smith	l ko 9	Glasgow
4 Apr	Terry Sloan	drew 8	Bath
10 May	Tommy Gibbons	w ko 7	Liverpool
4 Aug	Ted Duffy	w ko 2	Sunderland
10 Sep	Arthur Wright	w pts 8	Derby
29 Sep	Jimmy Jury	l rsc 3	Abergavenny
5 Nov	Johnny Fitzpatrick	drew 8	Derby
27 Nov	Benny Schaeffer	w ret 5	Grimsby
17 Dec	Dick Escott	w ret 7	Hartlepool
1946			
23 Jan	George Bridges	l pts 8	Fleetwood
28 Jan	Albert Ives	l pts 8	Derby
4 Feb	Reg Quinlan	l rsc 4	Walsall
17 Feb	Bob Bates	w pts 8	Durham
26 Feb	Mike Savage	w rsc 4	Grimsby
3 Jun	Jimmy Jury	l rsc 3	Hartlepool
27 Jun	Bob Burton	w pts 8	Newcastle
5 Aug	Billy Williams	w ret 4	Sunderland
8 Aug	Tommy Myers	w ret 6	Newcastle

10 Sep	Bob Bates	w pts 8	Durham
13 Sep	Harry Barrett	w ko 3	Middlesbrough
4 Nov	Dick Levers	l pts 8	Derby
15 Nov	Reg Mortimer	w ko 3	Middlesbrough
9 Dec	Pat Gorman	w ret 6	Hartlepool
1947			
13 Jan	Sam Darkie Sullivan	drew 8	Derby
30 Jan	Johnny Fitzpatrick	l dis 6	Newcastle
14 Feb	Tommy Myers	w ret 6	Middlesbrough
13 Mar	Billy Barton	drew 8	Hull
24 Mar	Sam Darkie Sullivan	drew 8	Derby
25 Apr	Billy Barton	w pts 8	Middlesbrough
23 Jun	Arthur Nutter	w ko 3	Hartlepool
21 Jul	Pat Gorman	w ret 6	Hartlepool
23 Oct	Mickey Green	w pts 8	Newcastle
24 Nov	Billy Kane	w pts 10	Newcastle
1948			
19 Jan	Billy Barton	l pts 8	Newcastle
12 Feb	George Daly	l pts 8	London
27 Feb	Dick Levers	drew 8	Sheffield
25 Mar	Billy Crane	w ko 4	Sheffield
26 Apr	Billy McDonald	l pts 8	Newcastle

20 May	Dick Levers	l pts 8	Ryhope
17 Jun	Johnny Fitzpatrick	w ko 3	Doncaster
7 Aug	Mickey Green	l dis 6	Ryhope
2 Sep	Ted Ansell	w pts 6	Hartlepool
18 Oct	Frank Parkes	l pts 8	Sutton-in-Ashfield
21 Oct	Tommy Barnham	l pts 8	London
4 Nov	Billy McDonald	l pts 10	Liverpool
22 Nov	Roy Sharples	l pts 4	Grimsby
1949			
10 Jan	Ezzie Reid	l pts 8	Grimsby
17 Jan	Johnny Fitzpatrick	w ko 1	Middlesbrough
31 Jan	Des Garrod	l pts 8	London
24 Feb	Billy Barton	l pts 8	Liverpool
16 Mar	Don Cameron	w dis 7	Glasgow
28 Mar	Mickey Green	l dis 2	Middlesbrough
2 May	Gerry Smyth	l pts 8	Belfast
14 Jul	Allen Tanner	l ret 2	Liverpool
17 Aug	Jimmy Trotter *Northern Area Lightweight title*	w pts 12	Sunderland
14 Oct	Les Rendle	l pts 8	Middlesbrough
14 Nov	Harry Brown	w ret 4	Newcastle

1950			
18 Jan	Jim Findlay	l pts 8	Paisley
14 Mar	Johnny Flannigan	l pts 8	Edinburgh
4 Apr	Algar Smith	l rsc 3	London
19 Jul	Harry Hughes	l pts 8	Coatbridge
9 Aug	Harry Hughes	l pts 8	Coatbridge
3 Oct	Johnny Flannigan	l pts 8	Edinburgh
16 Nov	Mickey Flannigan	l pts 8	Liverpool
11 Dec	Mias Johnson	w pts 8	Middlesbrough
1951			
5 Feb	Charlie Wisdom	w pts 8	Middlesbrough
2 Apr	Tony McTigue	l dis 4	Newcastle
26 Jul	Remo Odiroco	w rsc 4	London, Ontario
15 Oct	Eddie Nelson	l rsc 3	Detroit, U.S.A

CHAPTER SEVEN

BILLY HARDY

British Bantamweight Champion 1987-91
Commonwealth Featherweight Champion 1992-

When Billy Hardy hammered the reigning British bantamweight champion, Ray Gilbody, to defeat in three rounds, at St Helens, on 19 February 1987, he became the first Wearsider to win a British title and have the coveted Lonsdale Belt fastened round his waist. It is true that Silksworth-born Billy Thompson had won the British lightweight title, in 1947, but Thompson regarded himself as a Yorkshireman and he should be viewed as such. Billy Hardy not only won the British bantamweight title, he successfully defended it on four subsequent occasions, winning a Lonsdale Belt outright, and he went on to fight for European, World and Commonwealth titles. He has a proud ring record and his boxing career is not over: currently the Commonwealth featherweight champion, he still has time to add a European or World title to his laurels.

Billy was born in Castletown, on 15 September 1964, the second youngest in a family of 14; Billy has 10 sisters and three brothers.[1] His father worked in a local bakery and often had his leg pulled about his 'baker's dozen' family. There was always plenty of rough and tumble among the Hardy siblings and Billy learned to take care of himself.

Castletown was formerly a separate village on the north bank of the River Wear with its own colliery and ironworks, but by the time Billy Hardy was born it had been absorbed into Sunderland's boundaries and surrounded with new housing estates. He was educated at local schools - Castletown Junior and Castle View Comprehensive - and started boxing at the age of 10, at Hylton

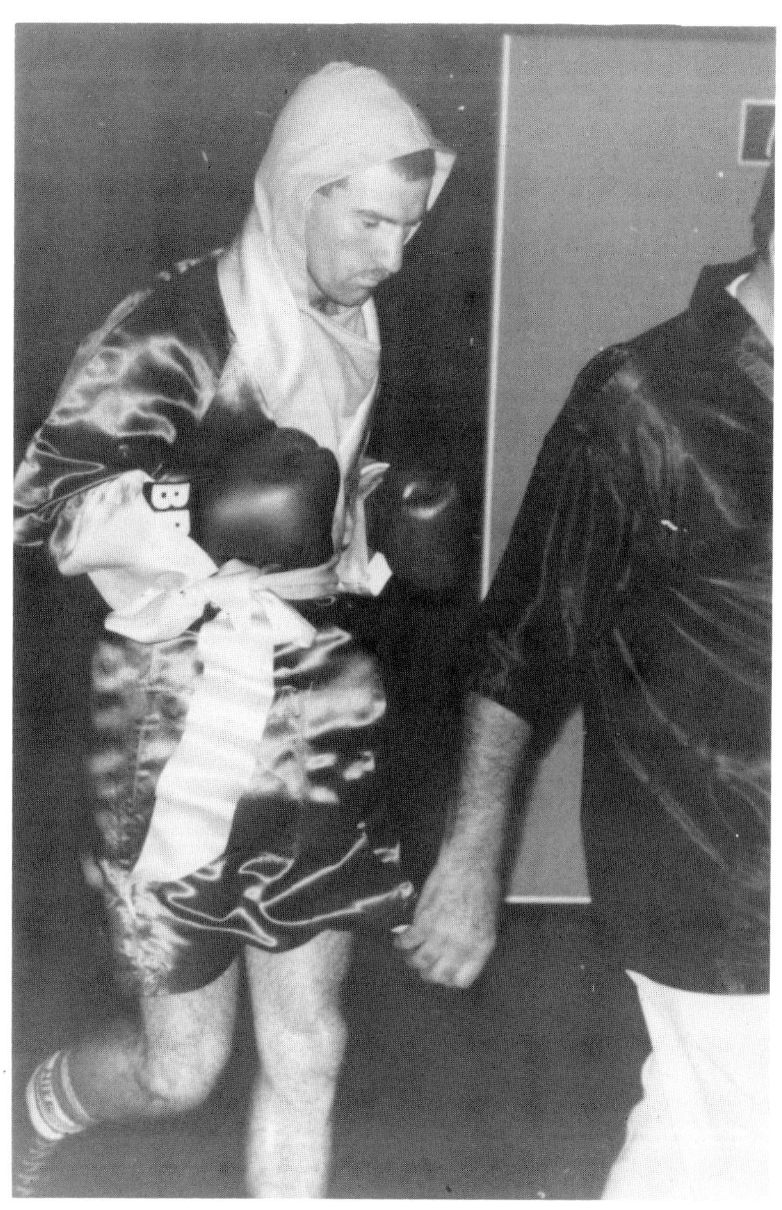

BILLY HARDY

Castle and Town End Farm Boys' Club. His other interest was in football, but it was boxing that became his passion. He now regrets that he did not work harder at school, but even as a boy it was his ambition to become a champion boxer and he devoted most of his time and energy to this end. The way up was not easy. Billy lost his first five fights as an amateur, and although he began to score some victories, he lost 50 out of his first 150 amateur fights. However, he had a good boxing instructor in Gordon Ibenson plus plenty of grit and determination. He won the Junior ABA title in 1981 and was the North East Counties bantamweight champion 1982-83.

In 1983, Billy Hardy faced a decision which most talented amateur boxers have to consider at some point: should he turn professional? He decided the time was ripe to make the move into the paid ranks and he answered an advert in a boxing magazine. Harry Holland, a London manager, was looking for fresh talent and Billy Hardy signed a year's contract with him and made the move to London. He had his first professional fight, on 21 November 1983, outpointing Kevin Downer over six rounds, at Eltham in South London.

Hardy chalked up eight consecutive wins in his first professional fights before he lost a narrow six rounds points decision to Roy Webb, at the National Sporting Club, in London, on 4 June 1984. The referee, Mike Jacobs, described the bout as the best six rounder he had ever handled, and the club's patrons threw in nobbins of £63. It has been said of Billy Hardy that, during this phase of his career, he was a typical 'nobbins fighter' - a popular all-action scrapper, ready to take on anybody.

After the Webb fight, Hardy came back with a points win over Les Walsh, at Gateshead. Then, on 10 October 1984, he was matched with Jorge Prentas, a featherweight from Costa Rica, at Shoreditch. Billy recalled: '*We were first on the bill and I was all*

ready to enter the ring when the officials discovered that Prentas didn't have the necessary permit to fight here. They had an emergency meeting and I was sitting around the dressing room while they sorted it out and two championship fights took place."'[2]
When Billy finally climbed into the ring, that night, his heart was not in it. He found it difficult to handle the heavier man's body punching and the referee stopped the contest in the fifth round. Billy's wife, Veronica, was expecting a baby at the time; they were both homesick, so after the fight they packed their bags and moved back to Sunderland, where Billy took a job as an electrician's mate.

Billy Hardy's boxing career hung in the balance at this point, as he considered retiring from the ring. Gordon Ibenson, Billy's boxing instructor from his amateur days, urged his protege to think carefully before he made up his mind. Billy rang up George Bowes at Hartlepool for his advice and George invited him to come and see him at his gym. John Feeney was at the gym and both he and George Bowes pressed Billy to keep on boxing.

> "*Once I got back in the gym,*" *recalled Billy,* "*I knew that I wanted to carry on. My contract with Harry Holland had expired, so I asked George if Mr Mancini could get me a couple of fights.*"
> Denni Mancini had watched Billy Hardy in action: "I could see there was genuine talent there," he said, later, "*I told him he had a choice - stay as a jobbing fighter, taking on anybody, anywhere, just for the money, or decide he was going to make something of his career.*"[3]

Billy Hardy made the choice and put himself under Mancini's management with George Bowes as his trainer.

Hardy's first bout under the Mancini regime was at the Albert Hall, on 12 February 1985, when he faced Ivor 'the engine' Jones in an eight round contest. Hardy let his aggressive opponent come to him and he met Jones with some crisp counter-punching which won him the decision on points. Jones had many fans and they clamoured for a return match and this took place over ten rounds, at Bethnal Green, two months later. This time Billy Hardy silenced Jones' supporters by winning decisively on points.

Two months later, Denni Mancini took a gamble which did not come off. It was a rare error of judgement on his part in his management of Hardy's career. Hardy was offered a fight with ex-European champion, Valeri Nati, in Florence, and Mancini accepted the match. Mancini's view was that Nati was on the slide and ready to be taken by a young, up- and-coming fighter. A victory over the former European champion would look good in Hardy's record and move him up the ratings. Unfortunately, Nati was not as far over the hill as Mancini believed, and the referee stopped the contest in the fourth round when Hardy injured his arm.

This defeat did not prove a setback in Billy's career, however. In October 1985, he was matched with Keith Wallace in a final eliminator for the British bantamweight title. It was an important fight to both men. Hardy was fighting his way up and to lose to Wallace would upset his championship hopes, Wallace, on the other hand, was a former Commonwealth title holder, who was on his way up the flyweight ranks when he was knocked out by Antoine Montero, in a European title fight. He had then moved up to the bantamweight class and wanted a crack at the British title. The fight was a see-saw struggle which saw both men on the canvas before Hardy smashed his way to victory in the seventh round.

After winning the eliminator, Hardy had to wait 16 months for his crack at the title, during which time the holder, Ray Gilbody, made two unsuccessful attempts at winning the European championship. Billy Hardy also suffered broken ribs, during a sparring session, and the cracked bones needed time to heal. Finally, the Gilbody-Hardy match was arranged to take place, at St Helens, on 19 February 1987. Gilbody had won three ABA titles and a Commonwealth bronze medal during his amateur years and he had beaten Hardy on his way to winning his third ABA title, in 1982. After turning professional, in the following year, Gilbody had gone on to win the British bantamweight title, in 1985. Billy Hardy defeated Gilbody inside three rounds. The champion was down four times in the first two rounds and was on his way to the canvas for the fifth time when the referee stopped the fight. After the bout, Denni Mancini paid a generous tribute to the Hartlepool trainer, George Bowes, who had turned out Hardy in peak condition.

Hardy had non-title fights against Rocky Lawlor and Brian Holmes, and was hoping to defend his title against John Hyland, in November 1987, when he had to postpone the bout in order to have a cartilage operation. The Hardy-Hyland fight was eventually fixed for 17 March 1988. Hardy had not fought for nine months but he had made a full recovery from his knee trouble. He was now working as a swimming pool attendant, at the Crowtree Leisure Centre, in Sunderland. Hardy's training programme consisted of getting up at 6 am and putting in some road work before starting the early shift at the leisure centre. After work, he motored down to the Hartlepool gym where he trained under the supervision of George Bowes. He returned to Sunderland for an evening meal and an early night in bed.

Billy Hardy had previously fought John Hyland in the quarter finals of the ABA championship, when the fight had been stopped in Hyland's favour. Hardy had always resented this decision because he felt he could have boxed on without any difficulty. It was a full house, at the Crowtree Leisure Centre, on the night of the championship fight. Hyland was a southpaw and he made the mistake of mixing it with the champion, who knocked him out with a left hook in the second round.

With the British title safely tucked away, Billy Hardy became interested in adding the European championship and, in November 1988, he met the holder, Italy's Vincenzo Belcastro, in Paola. It is notoriously difficult for foreign boxers to win in Italian rings and Hardy was adjudged to have lost narrowly on points. He secured a rematch with Belcastro, at Pavia, on 28 June 1989, and this time he gained a draw, but this meant that the Italian retained the European title.

In between his fights for the European title, Hardy successfully defended his British title against Ronnie Carroll, at the Crowtree Leisure Centre. Carroll was considered lucky to get a championship fight and Hardy was 4-1 on favourite to retain his title, but Carroll was keen to be the first Scot to win the British bantamweight title for 20 years and he turned out to be a much tougher proposition than many expected. He had a good opening round against Hardy, but then the Wearsider took the next four rounds with some good left jabs to the face and left hooks to the body. Carroll came back into the fight, in the middle rounds, urged on by his Scottish supporters in the crowd, but Hardy finished strongly and gained the verdict by $118^1/_2$ - $116^1/_2$ points. Ronnie Carroll won many cheers for his gritty performance. Hardy's victory gave him ownership of a Lonsdale Belt; and he finished 1989 with another British title defence, by knocking out Brian Holmes, in the first round.

The stage was now set for Billy Hardy's first world championship fight against Orlando Canizales for the IBF bantamweight title. The fight took place at the Crowtree Leisure Centre, on 24 January 1990. Apparently, Canizales thought his trip to England would be a way of picking up some easy money: he underestimated Billy Hardy and it nearly cost him his title. The fight was shown on ITV and many viewers were seeing

Billy Hardy v Orlando Canizales, Sunderland 24 January 1992

Sunderland's red-haired fighter for the first time and they were impressed by his performance.

The world title fight was preceded by two upheavals in Billy Hardy's life. In 1989, Billy went through the trauma of divorce from his wife, Veronica, with the court granting him access to his two children, Kirk and Danielle. A second split involved his trainer, George Bowes.

After the disappointment of the second Belcastro fight, Billy decided to take a holiday at his brother Colin's home, in South Africa. To keep in shape, Billy wandered into Richard Smith's gym, in Johannesburg, and he immediately hit it off with the ex-fighter, who had developed some controversial methods of training. Billy was impressed by Smith's unorthodox approach and decided that this was where he would train for his next big fight. '*George Bowes did a great job working with me*,' said Billy, '*and I'll always be grateful to him. But I felt it was time for a change.*'[4] Billy's manager, Denni Mancini, was philosophical about the switch: '*Managers and trainers can handle many boys in their time in this business, but a fighter has only one career, he has to do what he feels is best for him.*' In preparation for the Canizales fight, Hardy spent six weeks doing exercises, aerobics, swimming, running, chopping wood, mountain climbing and circuit training, before moving into the gym to begin sparring, bag punching and normal gym work.

Canizales was a strong, all-round fighter with a granite jaw and the capacity to deliver a good punch with either hand. He was a Hispanic who had come up the hard way in American rings. Several boxing correspondents rated him, pound for pound, the best champion of his time. He would clearly be no pushover for Hardy and so it proved.

Billy Hardy's fight with Orlando Canizales was rated Contest of the Year, in the Annual British Boxing Awards. Billy Hardy started confidently enough, but a Canizales right hook got through his guard and warned him that the Texan packed a heavy punch. In rounds two and three, Hardy scored and successfully kept out of the champion's range, but Canizales began to find his man, in the fourth, and Hardy was on the receiving end of some hard punches. The Wearsider came out fighting, in the fifth round, and he forced Canizales back on the ropes with an overhand right smash. The two men traded punches, in the sixth, and Hardy sustained a cut over his left eye. Canizales saw his chance and he opened up, in the next round, but his right eye took a knock, and in the following round a punch on his left eye made it swell. Both of the champion's eyes were puffed up and his vision was impaired but he still managed to deliver a left hook to Hardy's body which forced the Wearsider to drop on one knee and take a count of eight. Both men were prepared to slug it out and, in rounds eleven and twelve, Mancini urged Hardy to keep moving forward to clinch a decision. Many of those watching the bout - in the stadium and on television - believed that Hardy had done enough to win, but Canizales retained the title on a split decision. Italian judge, Walter Cavalieri, turned in a score of 115-114 for Canizales, American judge, Richard Murray, saw Canizales the winner, 115-113, while Britain's Dave Parris cast his vote for Hardy 116-113.

Billy had lost narrowly - and many considered him unfortunate to lose - however, there was no help for it but to keep fighting until he got another chance of lifting the world title. In May 1990, he halted Mexico's Miguel Pequeno, in four rounds, at Stockton, and, in November 1990, he defended his British title against Ronnie Carroll. Carroll had taken Hardy all the way at their previous meeting, but this time round Hardy gave the Scot a good pasting, prompting the referee to stop the contest, in the eighth round, with Carroll helpless on the ropes.

The return match with Canizales was arranged for 4 May 1991, at Laredo, Texas, and Billy Hardy was fixed up with a warm-up fight against Mexico's Francisco Ortiz, at the Crowtree Leisure Centre, on 28 February 1991. Ortiz was a tough experienced fighter who had fought most of his bouts in Mexico City and Acapulco, where the local fight fans demand plenty of action. He had recently been outpointed by the champion, Canizales, in a non-title fight contest, at Las Vegas, and therefore it would be instructive to see how Hardy would cope with him. Billy Hardy did better than the champion and put Ortiz down for five counts before the referee stopped the fight, in the seventh round.

After a week's rest, Hardy jetted off to South Africa to get into training for his second world title match with Canizales. He spent six weeks in South Africa before flying to Florida where he worked out at Mickey Duff's gym, spending the ten days before the fight in light training at the La Posado Hotel, in Laredo.

Hardy's second fight with Canizales promised to be tougher than the first. Canizales would not make the mistake of underestimating Hardy as he had done in their first bout. This was the first world championship fight to be staged in Laredo and it was a big event in the life of the border town. Canizales, a Texan of Mexican ancestry, would be fighting before a home crowd and many Mexican supporters would be pouring across the border to cheer him on. Furthermore, the fight would take place in the open air under hot and humid conditions which were unfamiliar to Hardy. Hardy would have to be at his fighting best on the day.

Billy Hardy's share of the purse was 25 per cent, which, after deductions, came to £7,000.[5] A group of North Eastern businessmen and supporters had raised £4,000 to help cover Hardy's training expenses in South Africa and Florida. Whatever else he has achieved, Billy Hardy has never made a lot of money out of boxing. For a fight at the Crowtree Leisure Centre, he might be paid £3,000, but after paying his manager's and trainer's fees, income tax, Boxing Board levy and covered the training expenses, he would be lucky to come out with £1,000.[6] Therefore, fighting three times a year did not provide him with a large income from boxing and he needed his job at the leisure centre to make ends meet.

The fight took place under a blazing sun, at 4 pm Texan time, before a crowd of 7,000, packed into the open-air arena in the grounds of the Laredo Civic Centre. Hardy was a bit tense in the opening rounds and, in the third round, a left hook from Canizales sent him somersaulting across the ring to land on his back, where he took a mandatory count of eight. Back on his feet, he held on grimly and recovered sufficiently to win the sixth and seventh rounds. In the eighth round, Canizales was beginning to tire and it looked as though Billy Hardy could turn the fight his way, when the champion caught him with another left hook. Hardy took the full count stretched out on the canvas. There were no excuses, after the fight, no blaming the heat and humidity or anything else for his defeat. "*I felt alright physically,*" said Hardy, "*I merely got caught by a great champion.*"[7]

On his return from the USA, Billy said that he would take a month's break from boxing and then get back into training with a view to getting another shot at the European title. His manager, Denni Mancini, arranged for him to meet the Texan, Mario Lozan, at the Crowtree Leisure Centre, on 5 September 1991, with the prospect of following up with a fight against Thierry Jacob of France for the European title. Then, on 19 August 1991, Billy Hardy announced that he was retiring from the ring. Denni Mancini said: "*Billy's had a problem with motivation for some time. Now, he's finally told me he can't motivate himself to continue boxing. I tried to talk him out of quitting. I told him, if he came through the European championship fight, he'd be on to something substantial. He tried to carry on training for a while, but then he came back to me and said he couldn't go on. With the Jacob fight coming up, things were starting to look good again, but he's the one who takes the punches and any decision on his future must be his. It might be a shock to some people that he's quitting, but not to anyone who knows him well. He's his own man. We've had a wonderful run together. Billy had five title wins, plus two challenges for the World and European titles. It's sad if it's over, but I'll look back on the wonderful times and the wonderful achievements we've had."*[8]

That could have been the end of the Billy Hardy story, but, on 1 January 1992, Billy announced that he was making a come-back, just four months after quitting the ring. " *What the retirement means is that I've had a break. I switched off and relaxed and now I'm ready again.* " A twist in his announcement was that he had broken with his manager, Denni Mancini. " *Denni and I were good for each other, but the partnership has gone stale. He won't release me from my contract, which still has 15 months to run. Denni wants money to release me and I can't afford that. He can't stop me from boxing. But he's entitled to 25 per cent of what I earn while I'm under contract. If that's the way Denni wants to operate, then that's how it will have to be. I'm not going to get involved with any other manager. I intend to look after my own affairs."*[9]

Billy Hardy's first come-back fight was against Chris Clarkson, at the McEwan Centre, Houghton-le-Spring, on 3 March 1992 - the first time this venue had been used for boxing. Clarkson was a gritty Yorkshireman who held the Central Area bantamweight and featherweight titles, and he could be expected to give Hardy a stiff test on what the fight programme described as Hardy's 'Last Crusade'. He started the bout looking a trifle ring-rusty but he got into his stride in the second round and dictated the rest of the fight, stopping Clarkson in the fifth round.

Billy Hardy v Ricky Rayner, Sunderland 7 October 1992

Another twist in Billy Hardy's career came in July 1992, when it was announced that he had signed a new three year contract with Denni Mancini and Mickey Duff. Two months later, Billy Hardy was matched with Australia's Rick Rayner for the vacant Commonwealth featherweight championship, at the Crowtree Leisure Centre, on 7 October.

Rick Rayner was the 21 year old Australian featherweight champion, with only eight professional fights behind him. The boxer from Sydney was something of an unknown quantity in Britain. He stood three inches taller than Hardy and weighed in at nine stone, with Hardy half a pound lighter. Billy Hardy was the favourite to win: he had the edge in experience, but Rayner was young and strong, and no-one was quite sure how good he was. John Gibson, sports editor of the *Newcastle Evening Chronicle*, speculated on whether Hardy still had the will to win, and concluded that he had.[10] Billy Hardy felt he was in a 'no win' situation: "*If I win in the first couple of rounds, everyone will say Rayner didn't deserve to get the fight. If I lose, everyone will say I'm finished,*" and he insisted that his old appetite for the game had returned.[11]

The championship fight night proved to be another great occasion at a packed Crowtree Leisure Centre. Billy Hardy entered the ring to the strains of 'Eye of the Tiger' and received a tumultuous reception from the crowd. He looked strong at his new weight, alongside the lanky Australian.

Hardy took the fight to Rayner from the opening bell. Rayner failed to use his longer reach to best advantage. Billy Hardy drew him into counter-punching and this enabled the Wearsider to move in close and deliver his punches. Rayner was no pushover, however, and stood up well to Hardy's attacks. He suffered a cut eye, in the third round, and Hardy dropped him for a short count, taken on one knee, in the fourth round. The fifth round proved to

Denni Mancini works on Billy Hardy between rounds while Mickey Duff looks on. Sunderland 7 October 1992

be Rayner's best and it was later revealed that Hardy had injured his right hand, in the previous round. After the fight, Billy explained: "*It happened in the fourth. I felt my hand go and tried to fight on in the fifth, one-handed. But that was no good and I decided to grit my teeth and just get on with it.*"[12]

There was a four minute interruption, at the end of the fifth round, when the ring floodlights went out and the rest of the contest was fought with the houselights switched on. After the resumption, Hardy's greater experience and superior ringcraft opened up a widening gap between the two men, as Hardy gradually got on top. He began to put together some good combinations of punches which shook the Australian, and 75 seconds into the tenth, the referee, Mickey Vann, stopped the fight to save Rayner from taking further punishment. Hardy was the new Commonwealth featherweight champion and he was presented with the Commonwealth champion's silver trophy. The next day, a visit to the hospital revealed that Hardy had broken two bones in his right hand, and that he would be out of action for at least six weeks. In fact, it was three months before Billy Hardy could use his hand on a punch-bag.

Billy Hardy's next fight was a defence of his Commonwealth title, at the Crowtree Leisure Centre, on 19 May 1993. His opponent was Barrington Francis. Francis was born in Jamaica but his family had moved to Canada when he was a young boy and he fought as a Canadian. He was a former holder of Commonwealth and WBF World titles and promised to be a formidable opponent. At the weigh-in, Hardy was found to be 2lb above the 9st limit and he disappeared for 45 minutes to sweat off the surplus weight.

Billy Hardy went on the offensive from the opening bell and had a good first round. In the second, however, the lanky Francis caught Hardy with a swinging right hand, on the side of the head, followed by a right hand chop. Hardy went down for a count of eight and when he rose, he was seen to be bleeding from a cut on his left ear. This incident was followed by a clash of heads and Hardy suffered a nasty cut over his left eye which bled for the remainder of the fight, although the injury did not seem to worry Hardy who kept moving forward on the attack throughout the contest. Francis was an awkward opponent: he used his long arms to provide a defensive screen and occasionally poked out a left and swung a right cross to Hardy's head. The middle rounds were fairly even, but in round eight, Hardy started to put together some good combinations of punches and Francis began to look tired. Billy had trained at the Hylton Castle gym, where he had started as a schoolboy boxer, and he seemed to have reserves of stamina to draw on as the fight progressed. Hardy kept up the pressure in the final rounds and ended the last round with a flurry of punches. Glasgow referee, Billy Rafferty, marked it $119^1/_2$ - 116 in Hardy's favour, although Harry Mullan, the editor of *Boxing News*, gave it to Hardy by a narrower margin and wrote: "*it was a triumph for old-fashioned, teeth-gritting courage as much as for skill or technique.*"[13]

Within a month, Billy Hardy was in action again, this time at the Decorum Pavilion, Hemel Hempstead, when his opponent was the tough Mexican southpaw, Angel Fernandez. Hardy spent the first three rounds feeling out the Mexican's style and then dominated the fight until the final bell, when he was awarded the verdict by $99^1/_2$ points to 96. In the same week, the European Boxing Union announced that it had nominated Billy Hardy to meet the winner of the clash between the European champion, Maurizio Stecco of Italy, and the challenger, Paul Hodkinson. The Stecco-Hodkinson contest was scheduled to take place in October 1993 and Billy Hardy was likely to get his crack at the European title early in 1994. In the meantime, Billy was to take a well-earned summer break, with the possibility of another fight in defence of his Commonwealth title taking place in the autumn.

CROWTREE SUNDERLAND

★ WEDNESDAY, 24th JANUARY, 1990 ★

Matchmaker: MICKEY DUFF *Assistant Matchmaker:* PADDY BYRNE

NATIONAL PROMOTIONS

in association with Deans & Deans
and the Borough of Sunderland

proudly present

IBF BANTAMWEIGHT CHAMPIONSHIP OF THE WORLD

ORLANDO

CANIZALES

(Houston, Texas) Champion

V

BILLY

HARDY

(Sunderland) Challenger

★ *PLUS FULL SUPPORTING PROGRAMME* ★

DOORS OPEN 7.00 PM COMMENCE 8.00 PM

★ TICKETS: ★ £100 ★ £75 ★ £50 ★ £25 ★

AVAILABLE FROM: Crowtree, Sunderland Tel: 091-514 2511. Frank Deans, South Shields Tel: 091-456 9492

Lyn Davison, Newcastle Tel: 091-276 1716
Sportspack, South Shields Tel: 091-456 7667
John White, South Shields Tel: 091-455 3151
Paddy Hallett, Newcastle Tel: 091-271 1239
Norman Fawcett, Newcastle Tel: 091-266 1285
Colemans Cafe, South Shields Tel: 091-456 1202
Bob Batey, Newcastle Tel: 091-272 3972
Tommy Conroy, Sunderland Tel: 091-567 6871
Nook Sports, South Shields Tel: 091-456 1464
John Spensley 0642-850717

But, whatever the future holds for Billy Hardy, his place in boxing history is assured, as the winner of British and Commonwealth championships plus the ownership of a Lonsdale Belt. He is a popular figure in his home town and takes a special interest in the activities of the local boys' boxing clubs. He often presents the prizes at boxing competitions and usually takes his Lonsdale Belt along to show the youngsters. Billy lives on the same estate where he was born, with his wife Allison and their daughter Alex Louise, and he works in a Sunderland sports shop, opposite the Crowtree Leisure Centre. Billy Hardy has remained close to his roots.

The Hylton Castle gym where Hardy trained
for his Commonwealth title fights

BILLY HARDY'S RING RECORD 1983-92

1983			
21 Nov	Kevin Downer	w pts 6	London
3 Dec	Brett Styles	w pts 6	London
1984			
21 Jan	Keith Ward	w pts 6	London
13 Feb	Johnny Mack	w rsc 6	London
1 Mar	Graham Kid Clarke	w pts 8	London
27 Mar	Glen McLaggon	w pts 6	London
6 Apr	Graham Kid Clarke	w rsc 7	London
25 Apr	Anthony Brown	w rsc 5	London
4 Jun	Roy Webb	l pts 6	London
6 Sep	Les Walsh	w pts 6	Gateshead
10 Oct	Jorge Prentas	l rsc 5	London
1985			
12 Feb	Ivor Jones	w pts 8	London
17 Apr	Ivor Jones	w pts 10	London
8 Jun	Valerio Nati	l rsc 4	Florence
10 Oct	Keith Wallace	w rsc 7	Alfreton
1986			
2 Jun	Rocky Lawlor	w pts 8	London

1987			
19 Feb	Ray Gilbody *British Bantamweight title*	w rsc 3	St Helens
23 Apr	Rocky Lawlor	w rsc 7	Newcastle
4 Jun	Brian Holmes	w pts 10	Sunderland
1988			
17 Mar	John Hyland *British Bantamweight title*	w ko 2	Sunderland
11 May	Luis Ramos	w rsc 2	London
29 Sep	Jose Gallegos	w rsc 4	Sunderland
2 Nov	Vincenzo Belcastro *European Bantamweight title*	l pts 12	Paola
1989			
14 Feb	Ronnie Carroll *British Bantamweight title*	w pts 12	Sunderland
29 Mar	Jose Soto	w pts 8	London
28 Jun	Vincenzo Belcastro *European Bantamweight title*	drew 12	Pavia
10 Oct	Brian Holmes *British Bantamweight title*	w ko 1	Sunderland

1990			
24 Jan	Orlando Canizales *IBF World Bantamweight title*	l pts 12	Sunderland
22 May	Miguel Paqueno	w rsc 4	Stockton
29 Nov	Ronnie Carroll	w rsc 8	Sunderland
1991			
28 Feb	Francisco Ortiz	w rsc 7	Sunderland
4 May	Orlando Canizales *IBF World Bantamweight title*	l ko 8	Laredo, Texas
1992			
3 Mar	Chris Clarkson	w rsc 5	Houghton-le-Spring
7 Oct	Ricky Rayner *Commonwealth Featherweight title*	w rsc 10	Sunderland
1993			
19 May	Barrington Francis *Commonwealth Featherweight title*	w pts 12	Sunderland
15 Jun	Angel Fernandez	w pts 10	Hemel Hempstead

NOTES

CHAPTER ONE: BOXING ON WEARSIDE

(1) Alan Brett and John Royal, *Old Pubs of Sunderland* (Sunderland 1993) p.14

(2) Fred Charlton, 'The furtive game of bare-knuckles', *Sunderland Echo* 15 January 1966.

(3) Joe Robinson, *Claret and Cross-Buttock or Rafferty's Prize Fighters* (London 1976) p.95

(4) Charlton op.cit.

(5) Fred Charlton, 'Collar and tie, the drill at Holmeside Stadium,' *Sunderland Echo* 12 March 1955, and G.J.Mellor, *Picture Pioneers: the story of the Northern Cinema 1896-1971* (Newcastle upon Tyne 1971) p.66

(6) *Sunderland Echo* 13 May 1920

(7) Fred Charlton, 'Boxing revived the Theatre Royal', *Sunderland Echo* 9 April 1966

(8) Fred Charlton, 'Promoter Simm scorned the sceptics', *Boxing News* 17 August 1949

(9) John Jarrett, 'Punchball starts the big boom', *Boxing News* 9 September 1977

(10) John Gibson, 'Boxing clever!', *Newcastle Evening Chronicle* 15 May 1991

CHAPTER TWO: JACK CASEY

(1) For a fuller treatment of Jack Casey, see: Archie Potts, *Jack Casey, the Sunderland Assassin* (Whitley Bay 1991) and Fred Charlton, 'The Jack Casey Story', *Boxing News* 1 July - 2 September 1955.

(2) For early part of Casey's career see Jack Casey, 'My fighting life', *Sunday Sun* 27 November - 19 December 1932, and Fred Charlton, 'Casey - a legend in his own lifetime', *Sunderland Echo* 6 November 1965.

(3) For references to Albert Johnson, see Michael Herbert, *Never counted out - the story of Len Johnson* (Manchester 1992) pp.24 and 51.

(4) Fred Charlton, 'Usworth pitman who twice defeated Jack Casey', *Sunderland Echo* 18 October 1969.

(5) Fred Charlton, 'He had a soft heart but his fists were rock hard', *Sunderland Echo* 12 March 1966.

(6) Fred Charlton, 'Casual Charlie McDonald could have been one of the greats', *Sunderland Echo* 16 December 1967.

(7) For comments on Casey v Thil fight see Peter Wilson, *Ringside Seat* (London 1950 edition) p.120

(8) The McAvoy - Casey fight was reported in the national and local press, but for accounts written later, see: Fred Charlton, 'A lightning blow from Jock McAvoy almost did the trick', *Sunderland Echo* 20 April 1968, and Jack Doughty, *The Rochdale Thunderbolt* (Stockport 1991) p.113

(9) The Harvey - Casey fight was reported in the national and local press, but for accounts written later, see: Fred Charlton, 'Casey was so close to British title', *Sunderland Echo* 20 November 1965, and Gilbert Odd, *Len Harvey - Prince of Boxers* (London 1978) pp 164-167.

(10) For this phase of Casey's career, see Fred Charlton 'A last fling then iron men retired', *Sunderland Echo* 27 November 1965.

(11) Patrick Myler, *The Fighting Irish* (Co.Kerry 1987) p.110.

CHAPTER THREE: DOUGLAS PARKER

(1) Fred Charlton, 'Parker lost first fight, but went on to develop a dynamic style', *Sunderland Echo* 20 January 1968.

(2) Fred Charlton, 'Douglas Parker hit town like a hurricane', *Sunderland Echo* 5 April 1955.

(3) Fred Charlton, 'Epic fights of Sharkey and Parker', *Sunderland Echo* 16 October 1963.

(4) Report in *Boxing* 9 December 1929.

(5) Fred Charlton, 'Parker never failed to pack the halls', *Sunderland Echo* 27 January 1968.

(6) Peter Wilson, *Ringside Seat* (1950 edition) pp 149-150.

CHAPTER FOUR: ROY MILLS

(1) Fred Charlton, 'Roy Mills: a boxing career over 20 years packed with memories', *Sunderland Echo* 19 March 1966, and 'Roy Mills had varied and flamboyant career', *Sunderland Echo* 1 November 1969, with additional information by Massie Wakenshaw et seq.

CHAPTER FIVE: TOM SMITH

(1) *Newcastle Evening Chronicle* 27 January 1968.

(2) Fred Charlton, 'Fighting Tom's 12 bill-topping years', *Sunderland Echo* 19 August 1967.

(3) Fred Charlton, 'Tom Smith - first fight for purse of 7/6d', *Sunderland Echo* 6 November 1965.

(4) For Billy Smith's boxing career, see: Fred Charlton, 'Billy Smith was never put down for a count', *Sunderland Echo* 9 April 1955, 'Billy Smith never on the canvas', *Sunderland Echo* 27 August 1966, 'Billy Smith - a born fighter but suffered many disappointments', *Sunderland Echo* 4 February 1967, and 'Billy Smith beat some of best in the land' *Sunderland Echo* 31 January 1970.

(5) Fred Charlton, 'How war delayed Smith's title battle' *Sunderland Echo* 26 August 1967.

(6) Billy Charlton, *A collection of poems and stories* (Gateshead, no date)

(7) Charlton, 'Tom Smith - first fight for a purse of 7/6d' op.cit.

(8) Fred Charlton, 'War in the air - and on the ground', *Sunderland Echo* 2 September 1967.

(9) Gilbert Odd, 'Long, lanky and so talented - that was Nella', *Boxing News* 3 September 1976.

(10) Charlton, 'War in the air - and on the ground', op.cit.

(11) ibid.

(12) ibid.

(13) Charlton, 'Tom Smith - first fight for a purse of 7/6d'. op.cit.

CHAPTER SIX: HUGHIE SMITH

(1) Fred Charlton, 'Hughie Smith - a Northern champion of longstanding', *Sunderland Echo* 3 January 1970, and interviews with Hughie Smith et seq.

CHAPTER SEVEN: BILLY HARDY

(1) Paul Tully, 'Hardy Billy in a new search for room at the top', *Newcastle Evening Chronicle* 14 March 1992, John Jarrett, 'Hardy's cast iron case for being the best', *Boxing News* 10 July 1987, and interview with Gordon Ibenson.

(2) John Jarrett, 'Billy Hardy chases his dream', *Boxing Outlook* April 1991.

(3) Simon Evan-Smith, 'Fighter profiles - Billy Hardy', Crowtree programme, 28 February 1991.

(4) Jarrett, 'Billy Hardy chases his dream', op.cit.

(5) Graham Robinson, 'World shot's a little earner' *Sunderland Echo* 2 May 1991.

(6) Graham Robinson, "Hardy: 'I can hit the top again'", *Sunderland Echo* 1 January 1992.

(7) John Gibson, 'A challenger's title dreams vanish in the heat', *Newcastle Journal* 6 May 1991, and Dean Lohuis, 'Too hot for Hardy', ***Boxing Monthly*** June 1991.

(8) Aidan Semmens, 'Billy Hardy quits boxing', *Sunderland Echo* 19 August 1991.

(9) Graham Robinson, 'Hardy ready to box again', *Sunderland Echo* 1 January 1992.

(10) John Gibson, 'It's now or never - Hardy must win or else...', *Newcastle Evening Chronicle* 3 October 1992, and 'Hardy hungry for success', *Newcastle Journal* 6 October 1992.

(11) Graham Robinson, 'Hardy has nothing to win but a title', *Sunderland Echo* 7 October 1992.

(12) John Gibson, 'Hardy to hospital' *Newcastle Evening Chronicle* 8 October 1992.

(13) Harry Mullan, 'Battling Billy keeps his hopes alive', *Boxing News* 28 May 1993.

SELECT BIBLIOGRAPHY

Books

Alan Brett and John Royal, *Old Pubs of Sunderland* (Sunderland 1993)

Billy Charlton, *A collection of poems and stories* (Gateshead)

Jack Doughty, *The Rochdale Thunderbolt* (Stockport 1991)

Michael Herbert, *Never counted out - the story of Len Johnson* (Manchester 1992)

Barry J Hugman, British Boxing Yearbooks (London 1985-93)

G.J.Mellor, *Picture Pioneers: the story of the Northern Cinema 1896-1971* (Newcastle upon Tyne 1971)

Patrick Myler, *The Fighting Irish* (Co.Kerry 1987)

Gilbert Odd, *Len Harvey: Prince of Boxers* (London 1978)

Archie Potts, *Jack Casey, the Sunderland Assassin* (Whitley Bay 1991)

Joe Robinson, *Claret and Cross-Buttock or Rafferty's Prize Fighters* (London 1976)

Peter Wilson, *Ringside Seat* (London 1950 edition)

Magazines

Boxing

Boxing Monthly

Boxing News

Boxing Outlook

Newspapers

Newcastle Evening Chronicle

Newcastle Journal

Sunderland Echo

ACKNOWLEDGEMENTS

I am grateful to the staffs of the British Newspaper Library, at Colindale, Newcastle Central Library, and the Sunderland Central Library for allowing me to consult their files of newspapers and periodicals. Photographs have been obtained from several sources and I should like to acknowledge the Sunderland section of the Tyne and Wear Museum Service, the Monkwearmouth Local History Society, John Brown, Frank Hutchinson, Les Simm, Hughie Smith and John Yearnshire; and to thank the editors of the *Newcastle Chronicle* and the *Sunderland Echo* for giving me permission to use press photographs. I should like to thank Vic Hardwicke and Miles Templeton for their assistance in compiling fight records, and Billy Charlton, Hughie Smith, Jack Todd and Massie Wakenshaw for recounting some of their memories of the fight game. Finally, I owe a huge debt to Leigh Clarke for preparing the manuscript for publication.